THE BOOK OF GENESIS

The Name Translation

Copyright © 2021 Christopher Monaghan

All rights reserved

The NTV text may be quoted in any form (written, visual, electronic or audio), up to and inclusive of five hundred (500) verses without express written permission of the publisher, providing the verses do not amount to a complete book of the Bible nor do the verses quoted account for twenty-five percent (25%) or more of the total text of the work in which they are quoted.

My team and I have strived for excellence and accuracy throughout this project and hope our efforts are pleasing in every way to our God the Father and our Lord Jesus Christ. In our own shortcomings, we present to you the Name Translation Version of the Bible. Please note that any errors in the text are the sole responsibility of the translator and if discovered notify me by emailing at chris@igateway.org.

ISBN: 9798738222252
Imprint: Independently published

Logo design by Art Painter
Cover design by Christopher Monaghan
Library of Congress Control Number: 2018675309
Printed in the United States of America

To my beloved wife, Debbie. Thank you for your unfailing support. Debra means both "an oracle or word from Yahweh" and "honeybee" in the Hebrew language. You are a mighty prophetic revivalist who channels a flow of honey to my path, sweetening my life, (Ezekiel 3:3) brightening my eyes, (1 Samuel 14:27) and strengthening my hands in the wilderness (Exodus 16:31). I love you so very much.

Special thanks to Sue Eason for her partnership in making this book a reality. Your sacrifice has been instrumental in advancing the kingdom of our God and raising up leaders in our generation.

Thank you to Karen Hardin, President of Priority PR Group & Literary Agency for her constant support and belief in this project.

Special thanks to Craig and Jan Hill of Family Foundations International. They are pioneers and godly examples in the kingdom of God. Craig has been instrumental in affirming to me the Biblical concept of using the meaning of names to help others discover their identity and destiny.

Thank you to Abiram Publications for providing one of most useful resources in completing this project that I discovered after I began my research. Abirampublications.com is an easy to use website for discovering the meaning of Biblical names.

And so grateful for our tribe at Gateway Church where Debbie and I pastor. Thank you for allowing me to follow my dreams and serve our community. You are the new giants in the land!

PREFACE

The Book of Genesis is the first book of the Hebrew Bible and the Christian Old Testament. Its Hebrew name is the same as its first word, Bereshit, which means, of the first, of the source or origin, or in the beginning. Genesis is His Story and the history of Yahweh reaching out to mankind. His interactions show us his passionate desire to fully reveal his nature to every man and women. Yahweh demands complete devotion from his prized possessions–everyone that he created. That is why he says, "For you will worship no other god: for Yahweh(*Jealous one*), whose name is Jealous, is a jealous God" (Exodus 34:14 NTV). Yahweh is one of the thousands of names translated for the reader in the text of the Name Translation Version(NTV).

In the NTV, the name meanings are derived from the root words of ancient languages – primarily from the Hebrew, Greek and Aramaic. Since many commentaries, word studies and name books vary in the origin of the name, my task was to prayerfully research and determine the best meaning for each name using a variety of sources. Next, I considered the events surrounding the naming of the person, place or object.

For instance, the name of the city Ramoth means "heights." The Hebrew root word for Ramoth is *ram* which means "to rise up or be high." Ramoth would be the plural for the Hebrew word *ram*. Now, if Ramoth was located on a hill, then the meaning of the name fits the description. However, if Ramoth were located in a valley, then an alternate root word would be considered. Someone once said, "If the name fits, then wear it!" And so it is with that deliberate process that these ancient name meanings were applied.

Sometimes the biblical names are homonyms– words that sound the same though have a different meanings. For example, the name Joseph was given to Isaac's and Rachel's next to last son because it sounded like the Hebrew word "to take away." But another root word connected with the name Joseph means "may He add." We receive insight into the situation at the time of his birth from the verse below.

> **"She conceived, gave birth to a son, and said, 'Our God has taken away my reproach.' She named him Joseph *(May He add)*, saying, 'May Yahweh *(Jealous one)* add another son to me' "** (Genesis 30:23-24).

There are almost 4,000 different proper names throughout the Bible and in each name, we discover a story. The NTV version allows readers to not only easily understand the meaning of every proper name, but to also understand the deeper connotation as it relates to the destiny of the person or location. It is a time-saving tool as the meaning is included right next to the name which eliminates the need to research via concordances, word studies and name books.

The translation used in the NTV is the World English Bible (WEB), which is a Modern English translation of the Holy Bible. The WEB was published in 2000 and is an updated revision of the American Standard Version (1901). I have made a few changes to the text of the WEB to make it more reader friendly and updated wording or terms that might not be easily understood by readers. At times it was also necessary to highlight the difference between a title and a name.

For example, the NTV treats the word "God" as a title instead of a name which you will see where "God" refers to His title and "Yahweh" refers to His name. This is similar to how we would read about King David in which "King" is his title and David is his name. In the New Testament as we read about Christ Jesus, "Christ" is His title and "Jesus" is His name. Where the Hebrew word "Elohim" is used, it is translated as "our God" instead of "God" to help communicate that "God" is a title, not a name.

Most theologians teach that there are many names for the God of the Bible. Though Yahweh and Jesus assume many different titles, Yahweh and Jesus each have only one personal name. Yahweh, whose name means "Jealous One" is the Father of Jesus. Jesus, whose name means, "Yahweh will save," is the son of Yahweh. The NTV clearly distinguishes between Yahweh and Jesus– though they share many of the same titles, they each have one specific name.

When Christ appears in the Old Testament, it is called a "Christophany." A Christophany notifies the reader that an undisclosed figure(Christ) will soon be revealed(phany). The NTV highlights the appearances of Jesus in the Old Testament for the reader.

In summary, the NTV was written with the belief that names are powerful and point us in the direction of our destiny. If we can discover the meaning of our name, we can better understand the purpose of our life. Remember, Zecharaiah's mouth was opened when he declared a name and Lazarus rose up at the sound of his name. Our very salvation is linked to a name– the name of Jesus. **"For there is salvation in no one else, for there is no other name under heaven that is given to man by which we must be saved"** (Acts 4:12). May the LORD bless your reading of the Name Translation Version and refresh you by His Spirit in the mighty name of Jesus.

Another disciple whom Jesus loved,

Christopher Monaghan

Janaury 7, 2021

INTRODUCTION

Names are more than just nice sounding words that identify one object from another. Names prophesy the connection between identity and destiny. The Bible reminds us that names have authority and so the naming of a child or location should be taken seriously–as the Bible says, **"For as his name is, so is he"** (1 Samuel 25:25). Research for the Name Translation Version (NTV) Bible project has been part of my ministry for over a decade. The more I have devoted myself to the study of names, the more I have become thoroughly convinced of their spiritual significance and how each name undeniably impacts lives and destinies.

The art of deciding on a name, whether for a child at birth or for something newly created, must not be undertaken without sacred inspiration. When a name is assigned correctly, a deep sense of satisfaction fills the room. It is no coincidence that the first job assigned to Adam was to give names to all the creatures.

The meaning of names in the Bible, whether of people, places or events–carries great significance. We know this because certain passages explain the meaning of the name and its importance to the reader. The NTV is the only version of the Bible which places the meaning of every proper name in parentheses next to the actual name. Hidden treasures are discovered as the meaning of each name is included directly in the text.

For instance, the apostle Paul reminded Philemon of the significance of his runaway slave when he included the meaning of the slave's name, Oneismus in his letter. Oneismus, means "useful." So the text actually reads as follows:

"Onesimus *(Useful)* who became my son while I was in

chains. Formerly he was useless to you, but now he has become useful both to you and to me" (Philemon 1:10-11).

Paul wrote that Onesimus was useful, just as his name foretold. (Although Philemon probably needed some convincing of that fact.) Paul connected the meaning of Onesimus's name purposefully to provide hope, encouragement and direction to the situation.

In Native American culture, babies are often named according to the timing and surroundings of the birth. For example, if a blackbird is seen flying overhead as the mother gave birth, the child might be named "Blackbird." If the harvest is coming in as the child is born, the child might be named "Harvest." This same process seems to be what they applied in biblical times when they named their children.

Unlike the way children are named in Western culture, biblical names are more spontaneously assigned at the time of birth. The day Rachel gave birth to her second son, **"...her soul was departing (for she was dying), she called his name Ben-oni; but his father called him Benjamin"** (Genesis 35:18). Rachel named him "Ben-Oni" meaning "son of my sorrow," but Jacob, the father, over-ruled her decision and changed it to Benjamin, which means "son of my right hand."

We also see where some meanings of names convey a negative connotation. The Hebrew name "Miriam" or often translated "Mary" comes from the root word "mara" which means bitter. To name someone "bitter" is not a wise choice, unless it is to signify a person who has authority in bitter situations. For instance, two women named Mary remained with Jesus during his entire crucifixion (Matthew 27:56). So, we see that those named Mary have the ability to stand with others through times of suffering.

A lesser known name is Jabez. The story of Jabez was made popular by author Bruce Wilkerson in his best-selling book, *The Prayer of Jabez* several years ago. The book describes someone who caused his mother much pain in birth. **"His mother named him Jabez***(Bringer of sorrow)*, **saying, 'Because I gave birth to him with sorrow.'**(1 Chronicles 4:9). Unfortunately, his mother chose to mark him forever with the remembrance of that hard day by naming him Jabez. As a result, anytime his name was spoken, he was reminded of the pain he caused his mother.

But one day, he cried out to our God to break the curse put upon him by his name. As he prayed, the blessing of our God was released and he was freed from one "bringing sorrow."

> ***Jabez(Bringer of sorrow)*** **called on the God of Israel(*Struggles with God*), saying, 'Oh that you would doubly bless me and enlarge my border! May your hand be with me and may you keep me from evil that I may not cause pain!' And our God granted him his request"** (1 Chronicles 4:10).

Scripture also gives us many examples of divinely mandated name changes. A name change signifies a transition into a new realm of authority and power. Abram's name was changed to Abraham prior to the birth of his son Isaac.

> "**Your name will no more be called Abram (*Exalted father*), but your name will be Abraham (*Father of nations*); for I have made you the father of a multitude of nations."** (Genesis 17:5).

Jacob wrestled with the God-angel-man prior to his name change.

> **"Your name will no longer be called Jacob *(Heel grabber)*, but Israel *(Struggles with God)*; for you have struggled with our God and men and have overcome"** (Genesis 32:28).

The meaning of heel grabber pointed to Jacob's nature of trickery which he often used to achieve his life goals. However, after this encounter, his name was changed to reveal his new nature. As Jacob, he struggled in the ways of man to get what he wanted, but as Israel, he struggled with his God to become an overcomer.

In the New Testament, Jesus changed the name of Simon to Peter as he declared the revelation of Jesus as the Christ. Jesus replied to Simon's Messianic confession:

> **"Blessed are you, Simon (*One who hears and obeys*) Bar-Jonah (*Son of a dove*), for flesh and blood has not revealed this to you, but my Father who is in heaven. I also tell you that you are Peter (*Stone*), and on this rock I will build my church and the gates of Hell will not prevail against it"** (Matthew 16:17-18).

Simon experienced a name change that prophesied his solid rock commitment to the declaration that Jesus is the Messiah. History confirms that Peter lived up to his name. Clement of Rome (35-99 C.E.) wrote, *"Peter... endured not one or two but many labors, and at last, having delivered his testimony, departed unto the place of glory due to him"* (1 Clement 5:4). Peter died delivering testimony of the Christ, like a cornerstone on which a building is built.

The Bible teaches us that the blessing of our God comes by having his name upon us. Yahweh gave Moses instructions on how to bless the people and to place His name upon them: **"Yahweh(*Jealous one*) bless you and keep you. Yahweh(*Jealous one*) make his face shine upon you and be gracious to you. Yahweh(*Jealous one*) lift up his face toward you and give you peace"** (Numbers 6:24-26). As this blessing is pronounced, the name of Yahweh is placed upon His people so that they may walk in peace. **"So will they place my name upon the children of Israel (*Struggles with God*); and I will bless them"** (Numbers 6:27). There is power in the name of Yahweh to bless us and power in the name of Jesus to save us. May your reading of the NTV open wide your spiritual eyes to the riches of sacred inspiration behind every name.

Another disciple whom Jesus loved,

Christopher Monaghan

January 7, 2021

GENESIS

CHAPTER 1

¹In the beginning, our God created the heavens and the earth. ²The earth was formless and empty. Darkness was on the surface of the deep and the Spirit of our God was hovering over the surface of the waters. ³Our God said, "Let there be light," and there was light. ⁴Our God saw the light and saw that it was good. Our God divided the light from the darkness. ⁵Our God called the light "day" and the darkness he called "night". There was evening and there was morning, the first day. ⁶Our God said, "Let there be an expanse in the middle of the waters, and let it divide the waters from the waters." ⁷Our God made the expanse and divided the waters that were under the expanse from the waters which were above the expanse; and it was so. ⁸Our God called the expanse "sky". There was evening and there was morning, a second day. ⁹Our God said, "Let the waters under the sky be gathered together to one place, and let the dry land appear"; and it was so. ¹⁰Our God called the dry land "earth", and the gathering together of the waters he called "seas". Our God saw that it was good. ¹¹Our God said, "Let the earth yield grass, herbs yielding seeds, and fruit trees bearing fruit after their kind, with their seeds in it, on the earth"; and it was so. ¹²The earth yielded grass, herbs yielding seed after their kind, and trees bearing fruit, with their seeds in it, after their kind; and our God saw that it was good. ¹³There was evening and there was morning, a third day. ¹⁴Our God said, "Let there be lights in the expanse of sky to mark the day from the night; and let them be for signs to mark seasons, days, and years; ¹⁵and let them be for lights in the expanse of sky to give light on the earth"; and it was so. ¹⁶Our God made the two great lights: the greater light to rule the day, and the lesser light to rule the night. He also made the stars. ¹⁷Our God set them in the expanse of sky to give light to the earth, ¹⁸and to rule over the day and over the night, and to divide the light from the darkness. Our God saw that it was good. ¹⁹There was evening and there was morning, a fourth day. ²⁰Our God said, "Let the waters abound with living creatures, and let birds fly above the earth in the open expanse of sky." ²¹Our God

created the large sea creatures and every living creature that moves, with which the waters swarmed, after their kind, and every winged bird after its kind. Our God saw that it was good. [22]Our God blessed them, saying, "Be fruitful, and multiply, and fill the waters in the seas, and let birds multiply on the earth." [23]There was evening and there was morning, a fifth day. [24]Our God said, "Let the earth produce living creatures after their kind, livestock, creeping things, and animals of the earth after their kind"; and it was so. [25]Our God made the animals of the earth after their kind, and the livestock after their kind, and everything that creeps on the ground after its kind. Our God saw that it was good. [26]Our God said, "Let us make man in our image, after our likeness: and let them have dominion over the fish of the sea, and over the birds of the sky, and over the livestock, and over all the earth, and over every creeping thing that creeps on the earth." [27]Our God created man in his own image. In the image of our God he created him; male and female he created them. [28]Our God blessed them. Our God said to them, "Be fruitful, multiply, fill the earth, and subdue it. Have dominion over the fish of the sea, over the birds of the sky, and over every living thing that moves on the earth." [29]Our God said, "Behold, I have given you every herb yielding seed, which is on the surface of all the earth, and every tree, which bears fruit yielding seed. It will be your food. [30]To every animal of the earth, and to every bird of the sky, and to everything that creeps on the earth, in which there is life, I have given every green herb for food;" and it was so. [31]Our God saw everything that he had made, and, behold, it was very good. There was evening and there was morning, a sixth day.

CHAPTER 2

¹The heavens, the earth, and all their vast array were finished. ²On the seventh day our God finished his work which he had done; and he rested on the seventh day from all his work which he had done. ³Our God blessed the seventh day, and made it holy, because he rested in it from all his work of creation that he had done. ⁴This is the history of the generations of the heavens and of the earth when they were created, in the day that our God Yahweh*(Jealous one)* made the earth and the heavens. ⁵No plant of the field was yet in the earth, and no herb of the field had yet sprung up; for our God Yahweh*(Jealous one)* had not caused it to rain on the earth. There was not a man to till the ground, ⁶but a mist went up from the earth, and watered the whole surface of the ground. ⁷God Yahweh*(Jealous one)* formed man from the dust of the ground and breathed into his nostrils the breath of life; and man became a living soul. ⁸God Yahweh*(Jealous one)* planted a garden eastward, in Eden*(Bliss)* and there he put the man whom he had formed. ⁹Out of the ground our God Yahweh *(Jealous one)* made every tree to grow that is pleasant to the sight, and good for food, including the tree of life in the middle of the garden and the tree of the knowledge of good and evil. ¹⁰A river went out of Eden*(Bliss)* to water the garden; and from there it was parted and became the source of four rivers. ¹¹The name of the first is Pishon*(Mouth)*: it flows through the whole land of Havilah*(Birthing)* where there is gold; ¹²and the gold of that land is good. Fragrant gum and onyx stone are also there. ¹³The name of the second river is Gihon*(Gushing forth)*. It is the same river that flows through the whole land of Cush*(Burning eyes)*. ¹⁴The name of the third river is Hiddekel*(Swift moving)*. This is the one which flows in front of Assyria*(Stepping forward)*. The fourth river is the Euphrates*(Fruitful)*. ¹⁵Our God Yahweh*(Jealous one)* took the man and put him into the garden of Eden*(Bliss)* to cultivate and keep it. ¹⁶Our God Yahweh*(Jealous one)* commanded the man, saying, "You may freely eat of every tree of the garden; ¹⁷but you will not eat of the tree of the knowledge of good and evil; for in the day that you eat of it, you will surely

die." ¹⁸God Yahweh*(Jealous one)* said, "It is not good for the man to be alone. I will make him a helper comparable to him." ¹⁹Out of the ground our God Yahweh*(Jealous one)* formed every animal of the field, and every bird of the sky, and brought them to the man to see what he would call them. Whatever the man called every living creature became its name. ²⁰The man gave names to all livestock, and to the birds of the sky, and to every animal of the field; but for man there was not found a helper comparable to him. ²¹God Yahweh*(Jealous one)* caused the man to fall into a deep sleep. As the man slept, he took one of his ribs, and closed up the flesh in its place. ²²God Yahweh*(Jealous one)* made a woman from the rib that he had taken from the man and brought her to the man. ²³The man said, "This is now bone of my bones, and flesh of my flesh. She will be called 'woman,' because she was taken out of man." ²⁴Therefore a man will leave his father and his mother, and will join with his wife, and they will be one flesh. ²⁵The man and his wife were both naked, and they were not ashamed.

CHAPTER 3

¹Now the serpent was more subtle than any animal of the field which our God Yahweh*(Jealous one)* had made. He said to the woman, "Has our God really said, 'You will not eat of any tree of the garden?'" ²The woman said to the serpent, "We may eat fruit from the trees of the garden, ³but not the fruit of the tree which is in the middle of the garden. Our God has said, 'You will not eat of it. You will not touch it, unless you die.'" ⁴The serpent said to the woman, "You will not surely die, ⁵for our God knows that in the day you eat it, your eyes will be opened, and you will be like our God, knowing good and evil." ⁶When the woman saw that the tree was good for food, and that it was a delight to the eyes, and that the tree was to be desired to make one wise, she took some of its fruit, and ate; and she gave some to her husband with her, and he ate it, too. ⁷Their eyes were opened, and they both knew that they were naked. They sewed fig leaves together and made coverings for themselves. ⁸They heard the sound of God Yahweh*(Jealous one)* walking in the garden in the cool of the day, and the man and his wife hid themselves from the presence of God Yahweh*(Jealous one)* among the trees of the garden. ⁹God Yahweh*(Jealous one)* called to the man, and said to him, "Where are you?" ¹⁰The man said, "I heard your voice in the garden, and I was afraid, because I was naked; and I hid myself." ¹¹Our God said, "Who told you that you were naked? Have you eaten from the tree that I commanded you not to eat from?" ¹²The man said, "The woman whom you gave to be with me, she gave me fruit from the tree, and I ate it." ¹³God Yahweh *(Jealous one)* said to the woman, "What have you done?" The woman said, "The serpent deceived me, and I ate." ¹⁴God Yahweh*(Jealous one)* said to the serpent, "Because you have done this, you are cursed above all livestock, and above every animal of the field. You will go on your belly and you will eat dust all the days of your life. ¹⁵I will put hostility between you and the woman, and between your offspring and her offspring. He will bruise your head, and you will bruise his heel." ¹⁶To the woman he said, "I will greatly multiply your pain in childbirth. In pain you will

bear children. Your desire will be for your husband, and he will rule over you." **¹⁷**To Adam(*Red*) he said, "Because you have listened to your wife's voice, and ate from the tree, about which I commanded you, saying, 'You will not eat of it,' the ground is cursed for your sake. You will eat from it with much labor all the days of your life. **¹⁸**It will yield thorns and thistles to you; and you will eat the herb of the field. **¹⁹**By the sweat of your face will you eat bread until you return to the ground, for out of it you were taken. For you are dust, and to dust you will return." **²⁰**The man called his wife Eve(*Life-giver*) because she would be the mother of all the living. **²¹**God Yahweh*(Jealous one)* made coats of animal skins for Adam(*Red*) and for his wife, and clothed them. **²²**God Yahweh*(Jealous one)* said, "Behold, the man has become like one of us, knowing good and evil. Now, unless he reach out his hand, and also take of the tree of life, and eat, and live forever." **²³**Therefore our God *Yahweh(Jealous one)* sent him out from the garden of Eden*(Bliss)* to till the ground from which he was taken. **²⁴**So he drove out the man; and he placed cherubim at the east of the garden of Eden*(Bliss)* and a flaming sword which turned every way, to guard the way to the tree of life.

CHAPTER 4

¹The man knew Eve*(Life-giver)* his wife. She conceived and gave birth to Cain*(Earned one)* and said, "I have gotten a man with the help of Yahweh*(Jealous one)*." ²Again she gave birth to Abel*(Vapor)*, the brother of Cain*(Earned one)*. Abel*(Vapor)* was a keeper of sheep, but Cain*(Earned one)* was a tiller of the ground. ³As time passed, Cain*(Earned one)* brought an offering to Yahweh*(Jealous one)* from the fruit of the ground. ⁴Abel*(Vapor)* also brought some of the firstborn of his flock and of its fat. Yahweh*(Jealous one)* respected Abel*(Vapor)* and his offering, ⁵but he did not respect Cain*(Earned one)* and his offering. Cain*(Earned one)* was very angry, and the expression on his face fell. ⁶Yahweh*(Jealous one)* said to Cain*(Earned one)*, "Why are you angry? Why has the expression of your face fallen? If you do well, will not it be lifted up? If you do not do well, sin crouches at the door. Its desire is for you, but you are to rule over it." ⁸Cain*(Earned one)* said to Abel*(Vapor)*, his brother, "Let's go into the field." While they were in the field, Cain*(Earned one)* rose up against Abel*(Vapor)*, his brother, and killed him. ⁹Yahweh*(Jealous one)* said to Cain*(Earned one)* "Where is Abel*(Vapor)* your brother?" He said, "I do not know. Am I my brother's keeper?" ¹⁰Yahweh*(Jealous one)* said, "What have you done? The voice of your brother's blood cries to me from the ground. ¹¹Now you are cursed because of the ground, which has opened its mouth to receive your brother's blood from your hand. ¹²From now on, when you till the ground, it will not yield its strength to you. You will be a fugitive and a wanderer in the earth." ¹³Cain*(Earned one)* said to Yahweh*(Jealous one)*, "My punishment is greater than I can bear. ¹⁴Behold, You have driven me out today from the surface of the ground. I will be hidden from Your face, and I will be a fugitive and a wanderer in the earth. Whoever finds me will kill me." ¹⁵Yahweh*(Jealous one)* said to him, "Therefore whoever slays Cain*(Earned one)* vengeance will be taken on him sevenfold." Yahweh*(Jealous one)* appointed a sign for Cain*(Earned one)*, so

that anyone finding him would not strike him. ¹⁶Cain(*Earned one*) left the presence of Yahweh(*Jealous one*) and lived in the land of Nod(*Wandering*), east of Eden(*Bliss*). ¹⁷Cain (*Earned one*) knew his wife. She conceived and gave birth to Enoch(*Dedicated*). He built a city, and called the name of the city Enoch (*Dedicated*) after the name of his son. ¹⁸To Enoch(*Dedicated*) was born Irad(*Fugitive*). Irad(*Fugitive*) became the father of Mehujael(*Clap of God*). Mehujael(*Clap of God*) became the father of Methushael(*I'm mortal, where is God?*). Methushael(*I'm mortal, where is God?*) became the father of Lamech(*One who reduces*). ¹⁹Lamech(*One who reduces*) took two wives: the name of the first one was Adah(*Adorned*), and the name of the second one was Zillah(*Darkened one*). ²⁰Adah(*Adorned*) gave birth to Jabal(*Conduit*), who was the father of those who dwell in tents and have livestock. ²¹His brother's name was Jubal(*Flow maker*), who was the father of all who handle the harp and pipe. ²²Zillah(*Darkened one*) also gave birth to Tubal-Cain(*Acquired flow of the world*) the forger of every cutting instrument of bronze and iron. The sister of Tubal-Cain(*Acquired flow of the world*) was Naamah(*Pleasant*). ²³Lamech(*One who reduces*) said to his wives, "Adah(*Adorned*) and Zillah(*Darkened one*), hear my voice. You wives of Lamech(*One who reduces*), listen to my speech, for I have slain a man for wounding me, a young man for bruising me. ²⁴If Cain(*Earned one*) will be avenged seven times, truly Lamech(*One who reduces*) seventy-seven times." ²⁵Adam(*Red*) knew his wife again. She gave birth to a son, and named him Seth(*One appointed*), saying, "for our God has given me another child instead of Abel(*Vapor*), for Cain(*Earned one*) killed him." ²⁶A son was also born to Seth(*One appointed*), and he named him Enosh(*Mortal man*). At that time men began to call on the name of Yahweh(*Jealous one*).

CHAPTER 5

¹This is the book of the generations of Adam(*Red*). In the day that our God created man, he made him in the likeness of our God. ²He created them male and female and blessed them. On the day they were created, he named them "Adam"(*Red*). ³Adam(*Red*) lived one hundred thirty years, and became the father of a son in his own likeness, after his image, and named him Seth(*One appointed*). ⁴The days of Adam(*Red*) after he became the father of Seth(*One appointed*) were eight hundred years, and he became the father of other sons and daughters. ⁵All the days that Adam(*Red*) lived were nine hundred thirty years, then he died. ⁶Seth(*One appointed*) lived one hundred five years, then became the father of Enosh(*Mortal man*). ⁷Seth(*One appointed*) lived after he became the father of Enosh(*Mortal man*) eight hundred seven years, and became the father of other sons and daughters. ⁸All of the days of Seth(*One appointed*) were nine hundred twelve years, then he died. ⁹Enosh(*Mortal man*) lived ninety years and became the father of Kenan(*Acquired*). ¹⁰Enosh(*Mortal man*) lived after he became the father of Kenan(*Acquired*), eight hundred fifteen years, and became the father of other sons and daughters. ¹¹All of the days of Enosh(*Mortal man*) were nine hundred five years, then he died. ¹²Kenan(*Acquired*) lived seventy years, then became the father of Mahalalel(*Praise to God*). ¹³Kenan(*Acquired*) lived after he became the father of Mahalalel(*Praise to God*) eight hundred forty years, and became the father of other sons and daughters ¹⁴and all of the days of Kenan(*Acquired*) were nine hundred ten years, then he died. ¹⁵Mahalalel(*Praise to God*) lived sixty-five years, then became the father of Jared(*One going down*). ¹⁶Mahalalel(*Praise to God*) lived after he became the father of Jared(*One going down*) eight hundred thirty years, and became the father of other sons and daughters. ¹⁷All of the days of Mahalalel(*Praise to God*) were eight hundred ninety-five years, then he died. ¹⁸Jared(*One going down*) lived one hundred sixty-two years, then became the father of Enoch(*Dedicated*). ¹⁹Jared(*One going down*)

lived after he became the father of Enoch*(Dedicated)* eight hundred years, and became the father of other sons and daughters. ²⁰All of the days of Jared(*One going down*) were nine hundred sixty- two years, then he died. ²¹Enoch(*Dedicated*) lived sixty-five years, then became the father of Methuselah(*When he is dead it will be sent*). ²²After the birth of Methuselah(*When he is dead it will be sent*), Enoch(*Dedicated*) walked with his God for three hundred years, and became the father of more sons and daughters. ²³All the days of Enoch(*Dedicated*) were three hundred sixty-five years. ²⁴Enoch(*Dedicated*) walked with our God, and he was not found, for our God took him. ²⁵Methuselah(*When he is dead it will be sent*) lived one hundred eighty-seven years, then became the father of Lamech(*One who reduces*). ²⁶Methuselah(*When he is dead it will be sent*) lived after he became the father of Lamech(*One who reduces*) seven hundred eighty-two years, and became the father of other sons and daughters. ²⁷All the days of Methuselah(*When he is dead it will be sent*) were nine hundred sixty-nine years, then he died. ²⁸Lamech(*One who reduces*) lived one hundred eighty-two years, then became the father of a son. ²⁹He named him Noah(*Bringer of comfort),* saying, "This one will comfort us in our work and in the toil of our hands, caused by the ground which Yahweh*(Jealous one)* has cursed." ³⁰After he became the father of Noah(*Bringer of comfort),* Lamech(*One who reduces*) lived five hundred ninety-five years and became the father of other sons and daughters. ³¹All the days of Lamech(*One who reduces*) were seven hundred seventy-seven years, then he died. ³²Noah was five hundred years old, then Noah(*Bringer of comfort*) became the father of Shem(*One who names*), Ham(*Intense*), and Japheth(*Formless expansion*).

CHAPTER 6

¹When men began to multiply on the surface of the ground, and daughters were born to them, ²the sons of our God saw that the daughters of men were beautiful, and they took any that they wanted for themselves as wives. ³Yahweh(*Jealous one*) said, "My Spirit will not strive with man forever, because he is also flesh; so his days will be one hundred twenty years." ⁴The Nephilim(*Ones who cause falling*) were in the earth in those days, and also after that, when the sons of our God came in to the daughters of men and had children with them. Those were the mighty men who were of old, men of renown. ⁵Yahweh(*Jealous one*) saw that the wickedness of man was great in the earth, and that every imagination of the thoughts of man's heart was continually only evil. ⁶Yahweh(*Jealous one*) was sorry that he had made man on the earth, and it grieved him in his heart. ⁷Yahweh(*Jealous one*) said, "I will destroy man whom I have created from the surface of the ground— man, along with animals, creeping things, and birds of the sky—for I am sorry that I have made them." ⁸But Noah(*Bringer of comfort*) found favor in the eyes of Yahweh(*Jealous one*). ⁹This is the history of the generations of Noah(*Bringer of comfort*): Noah(*Bringer of comfort*) was a righteous man, blameless among the people of his time. Noah(*Bringer of comfort*) walked with our God. ¹⁰Noah(*Bringer of comfort*) became the father of three sons: Shem(*One who names*), Ham(*Intense*), and Japheth(*Formless expansion*). ¹¹The earth was corrupt before our God, and the earth was filled with violence. ¹²Our God saw the earth, and saw that it was corrupt, for all flesh had corrupted their way on the earth. ¹³Our God said to Noah(*Bringer of comfort*), "I will bring an end to all flesh, for the earth is filled with violence through them. Behold, I will destroy them and the earth. ¹⁴Make a ship of gopher wood. You will make rooms in the ship, and will seal it inside and outside with pitch. ¹⁵This is how you will make it. The length of the ship will be three hundred cubits(*arm lengths*), its width fifty cubits(*arm lengths*), and its height thirty cubits(*arm lengths*). ¹⁶You

will make a roof in the ship, and you will finish it to a cubit(*arm length*) upward. You will set the door of the ship in its side. You will make it with lower, second, and third levels. ¹⁷I, even I, do bring the flood of waters on this earth, to destroy all flesh having the breath of life from under the sky. Everything that is in the earth will die. ¹⁸But I will establish my covenant with you. You will come into the ship, you, your sons, your wife, and your sons' wives with you. ¹⁹Of every living thing of all flesh, you will bring two of every sort into the ship, to keep them alive with you. They will be male and female. ²⁰Of the birds after their kind, of the livestock after their kind, of every creeping thing of the ground after its kind, two of every sort will come to you, to keep them alive. ²¹Take with you of all food that is eaten, and gather it to yourself; and it will be for food for you, and for them." ²²And Noah(*Bringer of comfort*) did this; he did all that our God commanded him.

CHAPTER 7

¹Yahweh(*Jealous one*) said to Noah(*Bringer of comfort*), "Come with all of your household into the ship, for I have seen your righteousness before me in this generation. ²You will take seven pairs of every clean animal with you, the male and his female. Of the animals that are not clean, take two, the male and his female. ³Also of the birds of the sky, seven and seven, male and female, to keep seed alive on the surface of all the earth. ⁴In seven days, I will cause it to rain on the earth for forty days and forty nights. Every living thing that I have made, I will destroy from the surface of the ground." ⁵Noah(*Bringer of comfort*) did everything that Yahweh(*Jealous one*) commanded him. ⁶Noah(*Bringer of comfort*) was six hundred years old when the flood of waters came on the earth. ⁷Noah(*Bringer of comfort*) went into the ship with his sons, his wife, and his sons' wives, because of the floodwaters. ⁸Clean animals, unclean animals, birds, and everything that creeps on the ground ⁹went by pairs to Noah(*Bringer of comfort*) into the ship, male and female, as our God commanded Noah(*Bringer of comfort*). ¹⁰After the seven days, the floodwaters came on the earth. ¹¹In the six hundredth year of the life of Noah(*Bringer of comfort*), in the second month, on the seventeenth day of the month, on the same day all the fountains of the great deep were burst open, and the sky's windows were opened. ¹²It rained on the earth forty days and forty nights. ¹³In the same day Noah(*Bringer of comfort*), and Shem(*One who names*), Ham(*Intense*), and Japheth(*Formless expansion*)—the sons of Noah(*Bringer of comfort*)—and the wife of Noah(*Bringer of comfort*) and the three wives of his sons with them, entered into the ship— ¹⁴they, and every animal after its kind, all the livestock after their kind, every creeping thing that creeps on the earth after its kind, and every bird after its kind, every bird of every sort. ¹⁵Pairs from all flesh with the breath of life in them went to Noah(*Bringer of comfort*) into the ship. ¹⁶Those who went in, went in male and female of all flesh, as his God commanded him; then Yahweh(*Jealous one*) shut him in. ¹⁷The flood was forty days on the earth.

The waters increased, and lifted up the ship, and it was lifted up above the earth. ¹⁸The waters rose, and increased greatly on the earth; and the ship floated on the surface of the waters. ¹⁹The waters rose very high on the earth. All the high mountains that were under the whole sky were covered. ²⁰The waters rose fifteen cubits higher, and the mountains were covered. ²¹All flesh died that moved on the earth, including birds, livestock, animals, every creeping thing that creeps on the earth, and every man. ²²All on the dry land, in whose nostrils was the breath of the spirit of life, died. ²³Every living thing was destroyed that was on the surface of the ground, including man, livestock, creeping things, and birds of the sky. They were destroyed from the earth. Only Noah(*Bringer of comfort*) was left, and those who were with him in the ship. ²⁴The waters flooded the earth one hundred fifty days.

CHAPTER 8

¹Our God remembered Noah(*Bringer of comfort*), all the animals, and all the livestock that were with him in the ship; and our God made a wind to pass over the earth. The waters subsided. ²The deep's fountains and the sky's windows were also stopped, and the rain from the sky was restrained. ³The waters continually receded from the earth. After the end of one hundred fifty days the waters decreased. ⁴The ship rested in the seventh month, on the seventeenth day of the month, on the mountain of Ararat(*Curse reversed*). ⁵The waters receded continually until the tenth month. In the tenth month, on the first day of the month, the tops of the mountains were visible. ⁶At the end of forty days, Noah(*Bringer of comfort*) opened the window of the ship which he had made, ⁷and he sent out a raven. It went back and forth, until the waters were dried up from the earth. ⁸He himself sent out a dove to see if the waters subsided from the surface of the ground, ⁹but the dove found no place to rest her foot, and she returned to him into the ship, for the waters were on the surface of the whole earth. He put out his hand, and took her, and brought her to him into the ship. ¹⁰He waited yet another seven days; and again he sent the dove out of the ship. ¹¹The dove came back to him at evening and, behold, in her mouth was a freshly plucked olive leaf. So Noah(*Bringer of comfort*) knew that the waters subsided from the earth. ¹²He waited yet another seven days, and sent out the dove; and she did not return to him anymore. ¹³In the six hundred first year, in the first month, the first day of the month, the waters were dried up from the earth. Noah(*Bringer of comfort*) removed the covering of the ship, and looked. He saw that the surface of the ground was dried. ¹⁴In the second month, on the twenty-seventh day of the month, the earth was dry. ¹⁵Our God spoke to Noah(*Bringer of comfort*), saying, ¹⁶"Go out of the ship, you, and your wife, and your sons, and your sons' wives with you. ¹⁷Bring out with you every living thing that is with you of all flesh, including birds, livestock, and every creeping thing that creeps on the earth, that they may breed abundantly in the earth, and be

fruitful, and multiply on the earth." ¹⁸Noah(*Bringer of comfort*) went out, with his sons, his wife, and his sons' wives with him. ¹⁹Every animal, every creeping thing, and every bird, whatever moves on the earth, after their families, went out of the ship. ²⁰Noah(*Bringer of comfort*) built an altar to Yahweh(*Jealous one*), and took of every clean animal, and of every clean bird, and offered burnt offerings on the altar. ²¹Yahweh(*Jealous one*) smelled the pleasant aroma. Yahweh(*Jealous one*) said in his heart, "I will not again curse the ground any more for man's sake because the imagination of man's heart is evil from his youth. I will never again strike every living thing, as I have done. ²²While the earth remains, seed time and harvest, and cold and heat, and summer and winter, and day and night will not cease."

CHAPTER 9

¹Our God blessed Noah(*Bringer of comfort*) and his sons, and said to them, "Be fruitful, and multiply, and replenish the earth. ²The fear of you and the dread of you will be on every animal of the earth, and on every bird of the sky. Everything that moves along the ground, and all the fish of the sea, are delivered into your hand. ³Every moving thing that lives will be food for you. As I gave you the green herb, I have given everything to you. ⁴But flesh with its life, that is, its blood, you will not eat. ⁵I will surely require your blood of your lives; at the hand of every animal I will require it. At the hand of man, even at the hand of every man's brother, I will require the life of man. ⁶Whoever sheds man's blood, his blood will be shed by man, for our God made man in his own image. ⁷Be fruitful and multiply. Increase abundantly in the earth, and multiply in it." ⁸Our God spoke to Noah(*Bringer of comfort*) and to his sons with him, saying, ⁹"As for me, behold, I establish my covenant with you, and with your offspring after you, ¹⁰and with every living creature that is with you: the birds, the livestock, and every animal of the earth with you, of all that go out of the ship, even every animal of the earth. ¹¹I will establish my covenant with you: All flesh will not be cut off any more by the waters of the flood. There will never again be a flood to destroy the earth." ¹²Our God said, "This is the token of the covenant which I make between me and you and every living creature that is with you, for perpetual generations: ¹³I set my rainbow in the cloud, and it will be a sign of a covenant between me and the earth. ¹⁴When I bring a cloud over the earth, that the rainbow will be seen in the cloud, ¹⁵and I will remember my covenant, which is between me and you and every living creature of all flesh, and the waters will no more become a flood to destroy all flesh. ¹⁶The rainbow will be in the cloud. I will look at it, that I may remember the everlasting covenant between your God and every living creature of all flesh that is on the earth." ¹⁷Our God said to Noah(*Bringer of comfort*), "This is the token of the covenant which I have established between me and all flesh that is on the

earth." ¹⁸The sons of Noah(*Bringer of comfort*) who went out from the ship were Shem(*One who names*), Ham(*Intense*), and Japheth(*Formless expansion*). Ham(*Intense*) is the father of Canaan(*Brought low*). ¹⁹These three were the sons of Noah(*Bringer of comfort*), and from these, the whole earth was populated. ²⁰Noah(*Bringer of comfort*) began to be a farmer, and planted a vineyard. ²¹He drank of the wine and got drunk. He was uncovered within his tent. ²²Ham(*Intense*), the father of Canaan(*Brought low*), saw the nakedness of his father, and told his two brothers outside. ²³Shem and Japheth(*Formless expansion*) took a garment, and laid it on both their shoulders, went in backwards, and covered the nakedness of their father. Their faces were backwards, and they did not see their father's nakedness. ²⁴Noah(*Bringer of comfort*) awoke from his wine, and knew what his youngest son had done to him. ²⁵He said, "Canaan(*Brought low*) is cursed. He will be a servant of servants to his brothers." ²⁶He said, "Blessed be Yahweh(*Jealous one*), the God of Shem(*One who names*). Let Canaan(*Brought low*) be his servant. ²⁷May God enlarge Japheth(*Formless expansion*). Let him dwell in the tents of Shem(*One who names*). Let Canaan(*Brought low*) be his servant." ²⁸Noah(*Bringer of comfort*) lived three hundred fifty years after the flood. ²⁹All the days of Noah(*Bringer of comfort*) were nine hundred fifty years, and then he died.

CHAPTER 10

¹Now this is the history of the generations of the sons of Noah(*Bringer of comfort*) and of Shem(*One who names*), Ham(*Intense*), and Japheth(*Formless expansion*). Sons were born to them after the flood. ²The sons of Japheth(*Formless expansion*) were: Gomer(*Bring to an end*), Magog(*From the roof*), Madai(*My measure*), Javan(*Swampy*), Tubal(*Flow of the world*), Meshech(*Drawn out*), and Tiras(*Desire*). ³The sons of Gomer(*Bring to an end*) were: Ashkenaz(*Spreading fire*), Riphath(*Dried fruit*), and Togarmah(*Bone breaker*). ⁴The sons of Javan(*Swampy*) were: Elishah(*God is salvation*), Tarshish(*White dove*), Kittim(*Crushers*), and Dodanim(*Leaders*). ⁵Of these were the islands of the nations divided in their lands, everyone after his language, after their families, in their nations. ⁶The sons of Ham(*Intense*) were: Cush(*Burning eyes*), Mizraim(*Double anxiety*), Put(*Gift*), and Canaan(*Brought low*). ⁷The sons of Cush(*Burning eyes*) were: Seba(*Drunkard*), Havilah(*Birthing*), Sabtah(*Breaking through*), Raamah(*Thunderous noise*), and Sabteca(*Circle of depression*). The sons of Raamah(*Thunderous noise*) were: Sheba(*Sworn promise*) and Dedan(*Moving forward*). ⁸Cush(*Burning eyes*) became the father of Nimrod(*Rebel*). He began to be a mighty one in the earth. ⁹He was a mighty hunter before Yahweh(*Jealous one*). Therefore it is said, "like Nimrod(*Rebel*), a mighty hunter before Yahweh(*Jealous one*)". ¹⁰The beginning of his kingdom was Babel(*Gate of God*), Erech(*To be long*), Accad(*Fortress*), and Calneh(*All of them*), in the land of Shinar(*Sharp city*). ¹¹Out of that land he went into Assyria(*Stepping forward*), and built Nineveh(*Dwelling of Descendants*), Rehobothir(*Spacious city*), Calah(*Full age*), ¹²and Resen(*Jaw*) between Nineveh(*Dwelling of descendants*) and the great city Calah(*Full Age*). ¹³Mizraim(*Double anxiety*) became the father of Ludim(*Twisted ones*), Anamim(*Responding waters*), Lehabim(*Flames*), Naphtuhim(*Openings*), ¹⁴Pathrusim(*Bits and Pieces*), Casluhim(*Protected boundary*) [which the Philistines(*Bringers of grief*) descended from], and Caphtorim(*Crowns*). ¹⁵Canaan(*Brought low*) became the father of Sidon(*Place to fish*) his firstborn, Heth(*Exhausted*), ¹⁶the Jebusites(*Ones who crush underfoot*), the

Amorites(*Talkers*), the Girgashites(*Dwellers on clay*), ¹⁷the Hivites(*Tent villager*), the Arkites(*Ones that gnaw*), the Sinites(*Those among thorns*), ¹⁸the Arvadies(*Refugees*), the Zemarites(*Those wearing two wool skins*), and the Hamathites(*Protected ones*). Afterward the families of the Canaanites(*Ones brought low*) were spread abroad. ¹⁹The border of the Canaanites(*Ones brought low*) was from Sidon(*Place to fish*)—as you go toward Gerar(*Dragged away*)—to Gaza(*Strong*)—as you go toward Sodom(*Burning*), Gomorrah(*Ones in Bondage*), Admah(*Earthy Red*), and Zeboiim(*United gathering*)— to Lasha(*Blinded by staring*). ²⁰These are the sons of Ham(*Intense*), after their families, according to their languages, in their lands and their nations. ²¹Children were also born to Shem(*One who names*), the father of all the children of Eber(*Crossed over*), the elder brother of Japheth(*Formless expansion*). ²²The sons of Shem(*One who names*) were: Elam(*Eternal*), Asshur(*Step forward*), Arpachshad(*One who releases*), Lud(*Twisted*), and Aram(*Elevated*). ²³The sons of Aram(*Elevated*) were: Uz(*Counsel*), Hul(*Great pain*), Gether(*Fear*), and Mash(*Drawn out*). ²⁴Arpachshad(*One who releases*) became the father of Shelah(*Sent out*). Shelah(*Sent out*) became the father of Eber(*Crossed over*). ²⁵To Eber(*Crossed over*) were born two sons. The name of the one was Peleg(*Division*), for in his days the earth was divided. His brother's name was Joktan(*He will be small*). ²⁶Joktan(*He will be small*) became the father of Almodad(*Immeasurable*), Sheleph(*Drawn out*), Hazarmaveth(*Death village*), Jerah(*Moon*), ²⁷Hadoram(High up thunder), Uzal(*One who goes away*), Diklah(*Palm tree*), ²⁸Obal(*Stripped*), Abimael(*My Father is God*), Sheba(*Drunk*), ²⁹Ophir(*Worn out*), Havilah(*Birthing*), and Jobab(*One who howls*). All these were the sons of Joktan(*He will be small*). ³⁰Their dwelling extended from Mesha(*Retreat*), as you go toward Sephar(*Census*), the mountain of the east. ³¹These are the sons of Shem(*One who names*), by their families, according to their languages, lands, and nations. ³²These are the families of the sons of Noah(*Bringer of comfort*), by their generations, according to their nations. The nations divided from these in the earth after the flood.

CHAPTER 11

¹The whole earth was of one language and of one speech. ²As they traveled east, they found a plain in the land of Shinar(*Sharp city*), and they lived there. ³They said to one another, "Come, let's make bricks, and burn them thoroughly." They had brick for stone, and they used tar for mortar. ⁴They said, "Come, let's build ourselves a city, and a tower whose top reaches to the sky, and let's make a name for ourselves, unless we be scattered abroad on the surface of the whole earth." ⁵Yahweh(*Jealous one*) came down to see the city and the tower, which the children of men built. ⁶Yahweh(*Jealous one*) said, "Behold, they are one people, and they have all one language, and this is what they begin to do. Now nothing will be withheld from them, which they intend to do. ⁷Come, let's go down, and there confuse their language, that they may not understand one another's speech." ⁸So Yahweh(*Jealous one*) scattered them abroad from there on the surface of all the earth. They stopped building the city. ⁹Therefore its name was called Babel(*Gate of God*), because there Yahweh(*Jealous one*) confused the language of all the earth. From there, Yahweh(*Jealous one*) scattered them abroad on the surface of all the earth. ¹⁰This is the history of the generations of Shem(*One who names*): Shem(*One who names*) was one hundred years old when he became the father of Arpachshad(*One who releases*) two years after the flood. ¹¹Shem(*One who names*) lived five hundred years after he became the father of Arpachshad(*One who releases*), and became the father of more sons and daughters. ¹²Arpachshad(*One who releases*) lived thirty-five years and became the father of Shelah(*Sent out*). ¹³Arpachshad(*One who releases*) lived four hundred three years after he became the father of Shelah(*Sent out*), and became the father of more sons and daughters. ¹⁴Shelah(*Sent out*), lived thirty years, and became the father of Eber(*Crossed over*). ¹⁵Shelah(*Sent out*), lived four hundred three years after he became the father of Eber(*Crossed over*), and became the father of more sons and daughters. ¹⁶Eber(*Crossed over*) lived thirty-four years, and became the father of Peleg(*Division*). ¹⁷Eber(*Crossed over*) lived four hun-

dred thirty years after he became the father of Peleg(*Division*), and became the father of more sons and daughters. ¹⁸ Peleg(*Division*) lived thirty years, and became the father of Reu(*Friend*). ¹⁹ Peleg(*Division*) lived two hundred nine years after he became the father of Reu(*Friend*), and became the father of more sons and daughters. ²⁰Reu(*Friend*) lived thirty-two years, and became the father of Serug(*Branch*). ²¹Reu(*Friend*), lived two hundred seven years after he became the father of Serug(*Branch*), and became the father of more sons and daughters. ²²Serug(*Branch*) lived thirty years, and became the father of Nahor(*Snorting*). ²³Serug(*Branch*) lived two hundred years after he became the father of Nahor(*Snorting*), and became the father of more sons and daughters. ²⁴Nahor(*Snorting*) lived twenty-nine years, and became the father of Terah(*Delay*). ²⁵Nahor(*Snorting*), lived one hundred nineteen years after he became the father of Terah(*Delay*), and became the father of more sons and daughters. ²⁶Terah(*Delay*) lived seventy years, and became the father of Abram(*Exalted father*), Nahor(*Snorting*), and Haran(*Hill dweller*). ²⁷Now this is the history of the generations of Terah(*Delay*). Terah(*Delay*) became the father of Abram(*Exalted father*), Nahor(*Snorting*), and Haran(*Hill dweller*). Haran(*Hill dweller*) became the father of Lot(*Covered*). ²⁸Haran(*Hill dweller*) died before his father Terah(*Delay*) in the land of his birth, in Ur(*Light*) of the Chaldees(*Flourishing mountains*). ²⁹Abram(*Exalted father*) and Nahor(*Snorting*) married wives. The name of the wife of Abram(*Exalted father*) was Sarai(*My princess*), and the name of the wife of Nahor(*Snorting*) was Milcah(*Queen*), the daughter of Haran(*Hill dweller*) who was also the father of Iscah(*She will discover*). ³⁰Sarai(*My princess*) was barren. She had no child. ³¹Terah(*Delay*) took Abram(*Exalted father*) his son, Lot(*Covered*) the son of Haran(*Hill dweller*), his son's son, and Sarai(*My princess*) his daughter-in-law, the wife of his son Abram(*Exalted father*). They went from Ur(*Light*) of the Chaldees(*Flourishing mountains*), to go into the land of Canaan(*Brought low*). They came to Haran(*Dry place*) and lived there. ³²The days of Terah(*Delay*) were two hundred five years. Terah(*Delay*) died in Haran(*Dry place*).

CHAPTER 12

¹Now Yahweh(*Jealous one*) said to Abram(*Exalted father*), "Leave your country, and your relatives, and your father's house, and go to the land that I will show you. ² I will make of you a great nation. I will bless you and make your name great. You will be a blessing. ³I will bless those who bless you, and I will curse him who curses you. All the families of the earth will be blessed through you." ⁴So Abram(*Exalted father*) went, as Yahweh(*Jealous one*) had told him. Lot(*Covered*) went with him. Abram(*Exalted father*) was seventy-five years old when he departed from Haran(*Dry place*). ⁵Abram(*Exalted father*) took Sarai(*My princess*) his wife, Lot(*Covered*) his brother's son, all their possessions that they had gathered, and the people whom they had acquired in Haran(*Dry place*), and they went to go into the land of Canaan(*Brought low*). They entered into the land of Canaan(*Brought low*). ⁶Abram(*Exalted father*) passed through the land to the place of Shechem(*Responsible*), to the oak of Moreh(*Teaching*). The Canaanites(*Ones brought low*) were in the land, then. ⁷Yahweh(*Jealous one*) appeared to Abram(*Exalted father*) and said, "I will give this land to your offspring." He built an altar there to Yahweh(*Jealous one*) who had appeared to him. ⁸He left from there to go to the mountain on the east of Bethel(*House of God*) and pitched his tent, having Bethel(*House of God*) on the west, and Ai(*Heap of ruins*) on the east. There he built an altar to Yahweh(*Jealous one*) and called on the name of Yahweh(*Jealous one*). ⁹Abram(*Exalted father*) traveled, still going on toward the Negev(*South*). ¹⁰There was a famine in the land. Abram(*Exalted father*) went down into Egypt(*Double anxiety*) to live as a foreigner there, for the famine was severe in the land. ¹¹When he had come near to enter Egypt(*Double anxiety*), he said to Sarai(*My princess*) his wife, "See now, I know that you are a beautiful woman to look at. ¹²It will happen, when the Egyptians(*Much anxious ones*) see you, that they will say, 'This is his wife.' They will kill me, but they will save you alive. ¹³Please say that you are my sister, that it may be well with me for your sake, and that my soul may live because of you." ¹⁴When Abram(*Exalted father*)

had come into Egypt(*Double anxiety*), Egyptians(*Much anxious ones*) saw that the woman was very beautiful. ¹⁵The princes of Pharaoh saw her, and praised her to Pharaoh; and the woman was taken into Pharaoh's house. ¹⁶He dealt well with Abram(*Exalted father*) for her sake. He had sheep, cattle, male donkeys, male servants, female servants, female donkeys, and camels. ¹⁷Yahweh(*Jealous one*) afflicted Pharaoh and his house with great plagues because of Sarai(*My princess*), the wife of Abram(*Exalted father*). ¹⁸Pharaoh called Abram(*Exalted father*) and said, "What is this that you have done to me? Why did not you tell me that she was your wife? ¹⁹Why did you say, 'She is my sister,' so that I took her to be my wife? Now therefore, see your wife, take her, and go your way." ²⁰Pharaoh commanded men concerning him, and they escorted him away with his wife and all that he had.

CHAPTER 13

¹Abram(*Exalted father*) went up out of Egypt(*Double anxiety*)—he, his wife, all that he had, and Lot(*Covered*) with him— into the Negev(*South*). ²Abram(*Exalted father*) was very rich in livestock, in silver, and in gold. ³He went on his journeys from the Negev(*South*) even to Bethel(*House of God*), to the place where his tent had been at the beginning, between Bethel(*House of God*) and Ai(*Heap of ruins*), ⁴to the place of the altar, which he had made there at the first. There Abram(*Exalted father*) called on th name of Yahweh(*Jealous one*). ⁵Lot(*Covered*) also, who went with Abram (*Exalted father*), had flocks, herds, and tents. ⁶The land was not able to bear them, that they might live together; for their substance was great, so that they could not live together. ⁷There was strife between the herdsmen of the livestock of Abram(*Exalted father*) and the herdsmen of the livestock of Lot(*Covered*). The Canaanites(*Ones brought low*) and the Perizzites(*Ones without boundaries*) lived in the land at that time. ⁸Abram(*Exalted father*) said to Lot(*Covered*), "Please, let there be no strife between you and me, and between your herdsmen and my herdsmen; for we are relatives. ⁹Is not the whole land before you? Please separate yourself from me. If you go to the left hand, then I will go to the right. Or if you go to the right hand, then I will go to the left." ¹⁰Lot lifted up his eyes, and saw all the plain of the Jordan(*Descending*), that it was well-watered everywhere, before Yahweh(*Jealous one*) destroyed Sodom(*Burning*) and Gomorrah(*Ones in bondage*), like the garden of Yahweh(*Jealous one*), like the land of Egypt(*Double anxiety*), as you go to Zoar(*Small*). ¹¹So Lot(*Covered*) chose the plain of the Jordan(*Descending*) for himself. Lot(*Covered*) traveled east, and they separated themselves one from the other. ¹²Abram(*Exalted father*) lived in the land of Canaan(*Brought low*), and Lot(*Covered*) lived in the cities of the plain, and moved his tent as far as Sodom(*Burning*). ¹³Now the men of Sodom(*Burning*) were exceedingly wicked and sinners against Yahweh(*J.alous one*) ¹⁴Yahweh(*Jealous one*) said to Abram(*Exalted father*), after Lot(*Covered*) was separated from him, "Now, lift up your eyes, and

look from the place where you are, northward and southward and eastward and westward, ¹⁵for all the land which you see, I will give to you, and to your offspring forever. ¹⁶I will make your offspring as the dust of the earth, so that if a man can number the dust of the earth, then your offspring may also be numbered. ¹⁷Arise, walk through the land in its length and in its width; for I will give it to you." ¹⁸Abram(*Exalted father*) moved his tent, and came and lived by the oaks of Mamre(*Revealed from seeing*), which are in Hebron(*Alliance*), and built an altar there to Yahweh(*Jealous one*).

CHAPTER 14

¹In the days of Amraphel(*Speaker of dark things*), king of Shinar(*Sharp city*), Arioch(*Lion-like*), king of Ellasar(*Prince of God*), Chedorlaomer(*Binder of sheaves*), king of Elam(*Eternal*), and Tidal(*For thanksgiving*), king of Goiim(*Nations*), ²they made war with Bera(*Gift*), king of Sodom(*Burning*), and with Birsha(*Strong*), king of Gomorrah(*Ones in bondage*), Shinab(*Father's tooth*), king of Admah(*Earthy red*), and Shemeber(*Known for strength*), king of Zeboiim(*United gathering*), and the king of Bela(*Devouring*) [also called Zoar(*Small*)]. ³All these joined together in the valley of Siddim(*Plowed field*) [also called the Melah(*Salt*) Sea]. ⁴They served Chedorlaomer(*Binder of sheaves*) for twelve years, and in the thirteenth year, they rebelled. ⁵In the fourteenth year Chedorlaomer(*Binder of sheaves*) came, and the kings who were with him, and struck the Rephaim(*To be sunken*) in Ashteroth-Karnaim(*Two horned star*), and the Zuzim(*Seasonal migrant*) in Ham(*Noisy*), and the Emim(*Terrifying one*) in Shaveh-Kiriathaim(*Double walled city on a level plain*), ⁶and the Horites(*Cave users*) in their Mount Seir(*Goat*), to El-Paran(*Glorious God*), which is by the wilderness. ⁷They returned, and came to En-Mishpat(*Spring of judgement*) [also called Kadesh(*Set apart*)], and struck all the country of the Amalekites(*Those who exhaust*), and also the Amorites(*Talkers*), that lived in Hazazon-Tamar(*Divided palm tree*). ⁸The king of Sodom(*Burning*), and the king of Gomorrah(*Ones in bondage*), and the king of Admah(*Earthy red*), and the king of Zeboiim(*United gathering*), and the king of Bela(*Devouring*) [also called Zoar(*Small*)] went out; and they set the battle in array against them in the valley of Siddim(*Plowed field*); ⁹against Chedorlaomer(*Binder of sheaves*) king of Elam(*Eternal*), and Tidal(*For thanksgiving*) king of Goiim(*Nations*), and Amraphel(*Speaker of dark things*) king of Shinar(*Sharp city*), and Arioch(*Lion-like*) king of Ellasar(*Prince of God*); four kings against the five. ¹⁰Now the valley of Siddim(*Plowed field*) was full of tar pits; and the kings of Sodom(*Burning*) and Gomorrah(*Ones in bondage*) fled, and some fell there, and those who remained fled to the hills. ¹¹They took all the goods of Sod-

om(*Burning*) and Gomorrah(*Ones in bondage*), and all their food, and went their way. **¹²**They took Lot(*Covered*), the nephew of Abram(*Exalted father*), who lived in Sodom(*Burning*), and his goods, and departed. **¹³**One who had escaped came and told Abram(*Exalted father*), the Hebrew(*One passing over*). At that time, he lived by the oaks of Mamre(*Revealed from seeing*), the Amorite(*Talker*), brother of Eshcol(*Cluster of grapes*), and brother of Aner(*Exile*); and they were allies of Abram(*Exalted father*). **¹⁴**When Abram(*Exalted father*) heard that his relative was taken captive, he led out his trained men, born in his house, three hundred and eighteen, and pursued as far as Dan(*One who judges*). **¹⁵**He divided himself against them by night, he and his servants, and struck them, and pursued them to Hobah(*Hiding place*), which is on the left hand of Damascus(*Carrier of life-blood*). **¹⁶**He brought back all the goods, and also brought back his relative, Lot(*Covered*), and his goods, and the women also, and the other people. **¹⁷**The king of Sodom(*Burning*) went out to meet him after his return from the slaughter of Chedorlaomer(*Binder of sheaves*) and the kings who were with him, at the valley of Shaveh(*Level plain*) [that is, the King's Valley]. **¹⁸**Mechizedek(*My King of righteousness*) king of Salem(*Complete peace*) brought out bread and wine: and he was priest of our God Most High. **¹⁹**He blessed him, and said, "Blessed be Abram(*Exalted father*) of our God Most High, possessor of heaven and earth: **²⁰**and blessed be our God Most High, who has delivered your enemies into your hand." Abram(Exalted father) gave him a tenth of all. **²¹**The king of Sodom(*Burning*) said to Abram(*Exalted father*), "Give me the people, and take the goods for yourself." **²²**Abram(*Exalted father*) said to the king of Sodom(*Burning*), "I have lifted up my hand to Yahweh(*Jealous one*) the God Most High, possessor of heaven and earth, **²³**that I will not take a thread nor a sandal strap nor anything that is yours, unless you should say, 'I have made Abram(*Exalted father*) rich.' **²⁴**I will accept nothing from you except that which the young men have eaten, and the portion of the men who went with me: Aner(*Exile*), Eshcol(*Cluster of grapes*), and Mamre(*Revealed from seeing*). Let them take their portion."

CHAPTER 15

¹After these things the word of Yahweh(*Jealous one*) came to Abram(*Exalted father*) in a vision, saying, "Do not be afraid, Abram(*Exalted Father*). I am your shield, your exceedingly great reward." ²Abram(*Exalted father*) said, "Lord Yahweh(*Jealous one*), what will you give me, since I go childless, and he who will inherit my estate is Eliezer(*My God helps*) of Damascus(*Carrier of lifeblood*)?" ³Abram(*Exalted father*) said, "Behold, to me you have given no children: and, behold, one born in my house is my heir." ⁴Behold, the word of Yahweh(*Jealous one*) came to him, saying, "This man will not be your heir, but he who will come out of your own body will be your heir." ⁵Yahweh(*Jealous one*) brought him outside, and said, "Look now toward the sky, and count the stars, if you are able to count them." He said to Abram(*Exalted father*), "So will your offspring be." ⁶He believed in Yahweh(*Jealous one*), who credited it to him for righteousness. ⁷He said to Abram(*Exalted father*), "I am Yahweh(*Jealous one*) who brought you out of Ur(*Light*) of the Chaldees(*Flourishing mountains*), to give you this land to inherit it." ⁸He said, "Lord Yahweh (*Jealous one*) how will I know that I will inherit it?" ⁹He said to him, "Bring me a heifer three years old, a female goat three years old, a ram three years old, a turtledove, and a young pigeon." ¹⁰He brought him all these, and divided them in the middle, and laid each half opposite the other; but he did not divide the birds. ¹¹The birds of prey came down on the carcasses, and Abram(*Exalted father*) drove them away. ¹²When the sun was going down, a deep sleep fell on Abram(*Exalted father*). Now terror and great darkness fell on him. ¹³He said to Abram(*Exalted father*), "Know for sure that your offspring will live as foreigners in a land that is not theirs, and will serve them. They will afflict them four hundred years. ¹⁴I will also judge that nation, whom they will serve. Afterward they will come out with great wealth, ¹⁵but you will go to your fathers in peace. You will be buried at a good old age. ¹⁶In the fourth generation they will come here again, for the iniquity of the Amorite(*Talker*) is not yet full." ¹⁷It came to pass that, when the sun went

down, and it was dark, behold, a smoking furnace, and a flaming torch passed between these pieces. ¹⁸In that day Yahweh(*Jealous one*) made a covenant with Abram (*Exalted father*), saying, "I have given this land to your offspring from the river of Egypt(*Double anxiety*) to the great river, the river Euphrates(*Fruitful*): ¹⁹the Kenites(*Ones in a nest*), the Kenizzites(*Hunters*), the Kadmonites(*Ones standing before God*), ²⁰the Hittites(*Terrorists*), the Perizzites(*Ones without boundaries*), the Rephaim(*To be sunken*), ²¹the Amorites(*Talkers*), the Canaanites(*Ones brought low*), the Girgashites(*Dwellers on clay*) and the Jebusites(*Ones who crush underfoot*)."

CHAPTER 16

¹Now Sarai(*My princess*), the wife of Abram(*Exalted father*), bore him no children. She had a servant, an Egyptian(*Much anxious one*), whose name was Hagar(*Fugitive*). ²Sarai said to Abram(*Exalted father*), "See now, Yahweh(*Jealous one*) has restrained me from bearing. Please go in to my servant. It may be that I will obtain children by her." Abram(*Exalted father*) listened to the voice of Sarai(*My princess*). ³Sarai(*My princess*), the wife of Abram(*Exalted father*), took Hagar(*Fugitive*) the Egyptian(*Much anxious one*), her servant, after Abram(*Exalted father*) had lived ten years in the land of Canaan(*Brought low*), and gave her to Abram(*Exalted father*) her husband to be his wife. ⁴He went in to Hagar(*Fugitive*), and she conceived. When she saw that she had conceived, her mistress was despised in her eyes. ⁵Sarai said to Abram(*Exalted father*), "This wrong is your fault. I gave my servant into your bosom, and when she saw that she had conceived, I was despised in her eyes. Yahweh(*Jealous one*) judge between me and you." ⁶But Abram(*Exalted father*) said to Sarai(*My princess*), "Behold, your maid is in your hand. Do to her whatever is good in your eyes." Sarai(*My princess*) dealt harshly with her, and she fled from her face. ⁷Angel-Yahweh(*Messenger of the Jealous one*) found her by a fountain of water in the wilderness, by the fountain on the way to Shur(*Raised wall*). ⁸He said, "Hagar(*Fugitive*), servant of Sarai(*My princess*), where did you come from? Where are you going?" She said, "I am fleeing from the face of my mistress Sarai(My princess)." ⁹Angel-Yahweh(*Messenger of the Jealous one*) said to her, "Return to your mistress, and submit yourself under her hands." ¹⁰Angel-Yahweh(*Messenger the Jealous one*) said to her, "I will surely multiply your offspring so that they cannot be numbered for multitude." ¹¹Angel-Yahweh(*Messenger of the Jealous one*)said to her, "Behold, you are with child, and will bear a son. You will call his name Ishmael(*God listens*), because Yahweh(*Jealous one*) has heard your affliction. ¹²He will be like a wild donkey among men. His hand will be against every man, and every man's hand against him. He will live opposite all of his brothers." ¹³She called on the name

of Yahweh(*Jealous one*) who spoke to her, "You are a God who sees," for she said, "Have I even stayed alive after seeing him?" ¹⁴Therefore the well was called Beer-Lahai-Roi(*A well of vision for life*). Behold, it is between Kadesh(*Set apart*) and Bered(*Hail*). ¹⁵Hagar(*Fugitive*) gave birth to a son for Abram(*Exalted father*). Abram(*Exalted father*) called the name of his son, whom Hagar(*Fugitive*) gave birth to, Ishmael(*God listens*). ¹⁶Abram (*Exalted father*) was eighty-six years old when Hagar(*Fugitive*) gave birth to Ishmael(*God listens*) to Abram (*Exalted father*).

CHAPTER 17

1When Abram(*Exalted father*) was ninety-nine years old, Yahweh(*Jealous one*) appeared to Abram(*Exalted father*), and said to him, "I am your God who is enough. Walk before me, and be blameless. **2** I will make my covenant between me and you, and will multiply you exceedingly." **3**Abram(*Exalted father*) fell on his face. Our God talked with him, saying, **4**"As for me, behold, my covenant is with you. You will be the father of a multitude of nations. **5**Your name will no more be called Abram(*Exalted father*), but your name will be Abraham(*Father of nations*); for I have made you the father of a multitude of nations. **6**I will make you exceedingly fruitful, and I will make nations of you. Kings will come out of you. **7**I will establish my covenant between me and you and your offspring after you throughout their generations for an everlasting covenant, to be a God to you and to your offspring after you. **8**I will give to you, and to your offspring after you, the land where you are traveling, all the land of Canaan(*Brought low*), for an everlasting possession. I will be their God." **9**Our God said to Abraham(*Father of nations*), "As for you, you will keep my covenant, you and your offspring after you throughout their generations. **10**This is my covenant, which you will keep, between me and you and your offspring after you. Every male among you will be circumcised. **11**You will be circumcised in the flesh of your foreskin. It will be a token of the covenant between me and you. **12**He who is eight days old will be circumcised among you, every male throughout your generations, he who is born in the house, or bought with money from any foreigner who is not of your offspring. **13**He who is born in your house, and he who is bought with your money, must be circumcised. My covenant will be in your flesh for an everlasting covenant. **14**The uncircumcised male who is not circumcised in the flesh of his foreskin, that soul will be cut off from his people. He has broken my covenant." **15**Our God said to Abraham(*Father of nations*), "As for Sarai(*My princess*) your wife, you will not call her name Sarai(*My princess*), but her name will be Sarah(*Daughter destined to rule*). **16**I will bless her, and moreover

I will give you a son by her. Yes, I will bless her, and she will be a mother of nations. Kings of peoples will come from her." ¹⁷Then Abraham(*Father of nations*) fell on his face, and laughed, and said in his heart, "Will a child be born to him who is one hundred years old? Will Sarah(*Daughter destined to rule*), who is ninety years old, give birth?" ¹⁸Abraham(*Father of nations*) said to our God, "Oh that Ishmael(*God listens*) might live before you!" ¹⁹Our God said, "No, but Sarah(*Daughter destined to rule*), your wife, will bear you a son. You will call his name Isaac(*Laughter*). I will establish my covenant with him for an everlasting covenant for his offspring after him. ²⁰As for Ishmael(*God listens*), I have heard you. Behold, I have blessed him, and will make him fruitful, and will multiply him exceedingly. He will become the father of twelve princes, and I will make him a great nation. ²¹But my covenant I establish with Isaac(*Laughter*), whom Sarah(*Daughter destined to rule*) will bear to you at this set time next year." ²²When he finished talking with him, our God went up from Abraham(*Father of nations*). ²³Abraham (*Father of nations*) took Ishmael(*God listens*) his son, all who were born in his house, and all who were bought with his money; every male among the men of the house of Abraham(*Father of nations*), and circumcised the flesh of their foreskin in the same day, as our God had said to him. ²⁴Abraham(*Father of nations*) was ninety-nine years old, when he was circumcised in the flesh of his foreskin. ²⁵Ishmael, his son, was thirteen years old when he was circumcised in the flesh of his foreskin. ²⁶In the same day both Abraham(*Father of nations*) and Ishmael(*God listens*), his son, were circumcised. ²⁷All the men of his house, those born in the house, and those bought with money from a foreigner, were circumcised with him.

CHAPTER 18

¹Yahweh(*Jealous one*) appeared to him by the oaks of Mamre(*Revealed from seeing*), as he sat in the tent door in the heat of the day. ²He lifted up his eyes and looked, and saw that three men stood opposite him. When he saw them, he ran to meet them from the tent door, and bowed himself to the earth, ³and said, "My lord, if now I have found favor in your sight, please do not go away from your servant. ⁴Now let a little water be fetched, wash your feet, and rest yourselves under the tree. ⁵I will get a morsel of bread so you can refresh your heart. After that you may go your way, now that you have come to your servant." They said, "Very well, do as you have said." ⁶Abraham(*Father of nations*) hurried into the tent to Sarah(*Daughter destined to rule*), and said, "Quickly prepare three seahs of fine meal, knead it, and make cakes." ⁷Abraham(*Father of nations*) ran to the herd, and fetched a tender and good calf, and gave it to the servant. He hurried to dress it. ⁸He took butter, milk, and the calf which he had dressed, and set it before them. He stood by them under the tree, and they ate. ⁹They asked him, "Where is Sarah(*Daughter destined to rule*), your wife?" He said, "See, in the tent." ¹⁰He said, "I will certainly return to you when the season comes round. Behold, Sarah(*Daughter destined to rule*) your wife will have a son." Sarah(*Daughter destined to rule*) heard in the tent door, which was behind him. ¹¹Now Abraham(*Father of nations*) and Sarah(*Daughter destined to rule*) were old, well advanced in age. Sarah(*Daughter destined to rule*) had passed the age of childbearing. ¹²Sarah laughed within herself, saying, "After I have grown old will I have pleasure, my lord being old also?" ¹³Yahweh(*Jealous one*) said to Abraham(*Father of nations*), "Why did Sarah(*Daughter destined to rule*) laugh, saying, 'Will I really bear a child, yet I am old?' ¹⁴Is anything too hard for Yahweh(*Jealous one*)? At the set time I will return to you, when the season comes round, and Sarah(*Daughter destined to rule*) will have a son." ¹⁵Then Sarah(*Daughter destined to rule*) denied it, saying, "I did not laugh," for she was afraid. He said, "No, but you did laugh." ¹⁶The men rose up from there, and looked toward Sodom(*Burning*).

Abraham(*Father of nations*) went with them to see them on their way. ¹⁷Yahweh(*Jealous one*) said, "Will I hide from Abraham(*Father of nations*) what I do, ¹⁸since Abraham(*Father of nations*) will surely become a great and mighty nation, and all the nations of the earth will be blessed in him? ¹⁹For I have known him, to the end that he may command his children and his household after him, that they may keep the way of Yahweh(*Jealous one*), to do righteousness and justice; to the end that Yahweh(*Jealous one*) may bring on Abraham(*Father of nations*) that which he has spoken of him." ²⁰Yahweh(*Jealous one*) said, "Because the cry of Sodom(*Burning*) and Gomorrah(*Ones in bondage*) is great, and because their sin is very grievous, ²¹I will go down now, and see whether their deeds are as bad as the reports which have come to me. If not, I will know." ²²The men turned from there, and went toward Sodom(*Burning*), but Abraham(*Father of nations*) stood yet before Yahweh(*Jealous one*). ²³Abraham(*Father of nations*) came near, and said, "Will you consume the righteous with the wicked? ²⁴What if there are fifty righteous within the city? Will you consume and not spare the place for the fifty righteous who are in it? ²⁵Be it far from you to do things like that, to kill the righteous with the wicked, so that the righteous should be like the wicked. May that be far from you. Should not the Judge of all the earth do right?" ²⁶Yahweh(*Jealous one*) said, "If I find in Sodom(*Burning*) fifty righteous within the city, then I will spare the whole place for their sake." ²⁷Abraham(*Father of nations*) answered, "See now, I have taken it on myself to speak to the Lord, although I am dust and ashes. ²⁸What if there will lack five of the fifty righteous? Will you destroy all the city for lack of five?" He said, "I will not destroy it, if I find forty-five there." ²⁹He spoke to him yet again, and said, "What if there are forty found there?" He said, "I will not do it for the forty's sake." ³⁰He said, "Oh do not let the Lord be angry, and I will speak. What if there are thirty found there?" He said, "I will not do it, if I find thirty there." ³¹He said, "See now, I have taken it on myself to speak to the Lord. What if there are twenty found there?" He said, "I will not destroy it for the twenty's sake." ³²He said, "Oh do not let the Lord be angry, and I will speak just once more. What if ten are found there?" He said, "I will not destroy it for the ten's sake." ³³Yahweh(*Jealous one*) went his way, as soon as he had finished communing with Abraham(*Father of nations*), and Abraham(*Father of nations*) returned to his place.

CHAPTER 19

¹The two angels came to Sodom(*Burning*) at evening. Lot(*Covered*) sat in the gate of Sodom(*Burning*). Lot(*Covered*) saw them, and rose up to meet them. He bowed himself with his face to the earth, ²and he said, "See now, my lords, please turn aside into your servant's house, stay all night, wash your feet, and you can rise up early, and go on your way." They said, "No, but we will stay in the street all night." ³He urged them greatly, and they came in with him, and entered into his house. He made them a feast, and baked unleavened bread, and they ate. ⁴But before they lay down, the men of the city, the men of Sodom(*Burning*), surrounded the house, both young and old, all the people from every quarter. ⁵They called to Lot(*Covered*), and said to him, "Where are the men who came in to you this night? Bring them out to us, that we may have sex with them." ⁶Lot(*Covered*) went out to them to the door, and shut the door after him. ⁷He said, "Please, my brothers, do not act so wickedly. ⁸See now, I have two virgin daughters. Please let me bring them out to you, and you may do to them what seems good to you. Only do not do anything to these men, because they have come under the shadow of my roof." ⁹They said, "Stand back!" Then they said, "This one fellow came in to live as a foreigner, and he appoints himself a judge. Now will we deal worse with you, than with them!" They pressed hard on the man Lot(*Covered*), and came near to break the door. ¹⁰But the men reached out their hand, and brought Lot(*Covered*) into the house to them, and shut the door. ¹¹They struck the men who were at the door of the house with blindness, both small and great, so that they wearied themselves to find the door. ¹²The men said to Lot(*Covered*), "Do you have anybody else here? Sons-in-law, your sons, your daughters, and whoever you have in the city, bring them out of the place: ¹³for we will destroy this place, because the outcry against them has grown great before Yahweh(*Jealous one*) that Yahweh(*Jealous one*) has sent us to destroy it." ¹⁴Lot(*Covered*) went out, and spoke to his sons-in-law, who were pledged to marry his daughters, and said, "Get up! Get out of this

place, for Yahweh(*Jealous one*) will destroy the city." But he seemed to his sons-in-law to be joking. ¹⁵When the morning came, then the angels hurried Lot(*Covered*), saying, "Get up! Take your wife, and your two daughters who are here, unless you be consumed in the iniquity of the city." ¹⁶But he lingered; and the men grabbed his hand, his wife's hand, and his two daughters' hands, Yahweh(*Jealous one) Who Causes Existence*) being merciful to him; and they took him out, and set him outside of the city. ¹⁷It came to pass, when they had taken them out, that he said, "Escape for your life! Do not look behind you, and do not stay anywhere in the plain. Escape to the mountains, unless you be consumed!" ¹⁸Lot(*Covered*) said to them, "Oh, not so, my lord. ¹⁹See now, your servant has found favor in your sight, and you have magnified your lovingkindness, which you have shown to me in saving my life. I cannot escape to the mountain, unless evil overtake me, and I die. ²⁰See now, this city is near to flee to, and it is a little one. Oh let me escape there [is not it a little one?], and my soul will live." ²¹He said to him, "Behold, I have granted your request concerning this thing also, that I will not overthrow the city of which you have spoken. ²²Hurry, escape there, for I cannot do anything until you get there." Therefore the name of the city was called Zoar(*Small*). ²³The sun had risen on the earth when Lot(*Covered*) came to Zoar(*Small*). ²⁴Then Yahweh(*Jealous one*) rained on Sodom(*Burning*) and on Gomorrah(*Ones in bondage*) sulfur and fire from Yahweh(*Jealous one*) out of the sky. ²⁵He overthrew those cities, all the plain, all the inhabitants of the cities, and that which grew on the ground. ²⁶But his wife looked back from behind him, and she became a pillar of salt. ²⁷Abraham(*Father of nations*) got up early in the morning to the place where he had stood before Yahweh(*Jealous one*). ²⁸He looked toward Sodom(*Burning*) and Gomorrah(*Ones in bondage*), and toward all the land of the plain, and looked, and saw that the smoke of the land went up as the smoke of a furnace. ²⁹When God destroyed the cities of the plain, our God remembered Abraham(*Father of nations*), and sent Lot(*Covered*) out of the middle of the overthrow, when he overthrew the cities in which Lot(*Covered*) lived. ³⁰Lot(*Covered*) went up out of Zoar(*Small*), and lived in the mountain, and his two daughters with him; for he was afraid to live in Zoar(*Small*). He lived in a cave with his two daughters. ³¹The firstborn said to the younger, "Our father is old, and there is not a man in the earth to come in to us in the way of all the earth. ³²Come, let's make our father drink wine, and we will lie with him, that we may preserve our father's family line." ³³They made their father drink wine that night: and the firstborn went in, and lay with her father. He did not know when she lay down, nor when she arose. ³⁴It came to pass on the next day, that the firstborn said to the younger, "Behold, I lay last night with my father. Let us make him drink wine again, tonight. You go in, and lie with him, that we may preserve our father's family line." ³⁵They made their father drink wine that night also. The younger went and lay with him. He did not know when she lay down, nor when she got up. ³⁶Thus both of daughters of Lot(*Covered*) were with child by their father. ³⁷The firstborn gave birth to a son, and named him Moab(*Unknown father*). He is the father of the Moabites(*Ones with unknown father*) to this day. ³⁸The younger also gave birth to a son, and called his name Ben-Ammi(*Son of my people*). He is the father of the children of Ammon(*Great people*) to this day.

CHAPTER 20

¹Abraham(*Father of nations*) traveled from there toward the land of the Negev(*South*), and lived between Kadesh(*Set apart*) and Shur(*Raised wall*). He lived as a foreigner in Gerar(*Dragged away*). ²Abraham (*Father of nations*) said about Sarah(*Daughter destined to rule*) his wife, "She is my sister." Abimelech(*My father is king*) king of Gerar(*Dragged away*) sent, and took Sarah(*Daughter destined to rule*). ³But our God came to Abimelech(*My father is king*) in a dream of the night, and said to him, "Behold, you are a dead man, because of the woman whom you have taken. For she is a man's wife." ⁴Now Abimelech(*My father is king*) had not come near her. He said, "Lord, will you kill even a righteous nation? ⁵Did not he tell me, 'She is my sister?' She, even she herself, said, 'He is my brother.' In the integrity of my heart and the innocence of my hands have I done this." ⁶Our God said to him in the dream, "Yes, I know that in the integrity of your heart you have done this, and I also withheld you from sinning against me. Therefore I did not allow you to touch her. ⁷Now therefore, restore the man's wife. For he is a prophet, and he will pray for you, and you will live. If you do not restore her, know for sure that you will die, you, and all who are yours." ⁸Abimelech(*My father is king*) rose early in the morning, and called all his servants, and told all these things in their ear. The men were very scared. ⁹Then Abimelech(*My father is king*) called Abraham (*Father of nations*), and said to him, "What have you done to us? How have I sinned against you, that you have brought on me and on my kingdom a great sin? You have done deeds to me that ought not to be done!" ¹⁰Abimelech(*My father is king*) said to Abraham(*Father of nations*), "What did you see, that you have done this thing?" ¹¹Abraham(*Father of nations*) said, "Because I thought, 'Surely the fear of God is not in this place. They will kill me for my wife's sake.' ¹²Besides, she is indeed my sister, the daughter of my father, but not the daughter of my mother; and she became my wife. ¹³When our God caused me to wander from my father's house, I said to her, 'This is your kindness which you will show to me. Everywhere that we go, say of me, "He is my

brother."'" ¹⁴Abimelech(*My father is king*) took sheep and cattle, male servants and female servants, and gave them to Abraham(*Father of nations*), and restored Sarah(*Daughter destined to rule*), his wife, to him. ¹⁵Abimelech(*My father is king*) said, "Behold, my land is before you. Dwell where it pleases you." ¹⁶To Sarah(*Daughter destined to rule*) he said, "Behold, I have given your brother a thousand pieces of silver. Behold, it is for you a covering of the eyes to all that are with you. In front of all you are vindicated." ¹⁷Abraham(*Father of nations*) prayed to our God. Our God healed Abimelech(*My father is king*), and his wife, and his female servants, and they gave birth to children. ¹⁸For Yahweh(*Jealous one*) had closed up tight all the wombs of the house of Abimelech(*My father is king*), because of Sarah(*Daughter destined to rule*), the wife of Abraham(*Father of nations*) wife.

CHAPTER 21

¹Yahweh*(Jealous one)* visited Sarah*(Daughter destined to rule)* as he had said, and Yahweh *(Jealous one)* did to Sarah*(Daughter destined to rule)* as he had spoken. ²Sarah*(Daughter destined to rule)* conceived, and bore to Abraham*(Father of nations)* a son in his old age, at the set time of which our God had spoken to him. ³Abraham*(Father of nations)* called his son who was born to him, whom Sarah*(Daughter destined to rule)* bore to him, Isaac*(Laughter)*. ⁴Abraham*(Father of nations)* circumcised his son, Isaac*(Laughter)*, when he was eight days old, as our God had commanded him. ⁵Abraham*(Father of nations)* was one hundred years old when his son, Isaac(Laughter), was born to him. ⁶Sarah*(Daughter destined to rule)* said, "Our God has made me laugh. Everyone who hears will laugh with me." ⁷She said, "Who would have said to Abraham*(Father of nations)*, that Sarah *(Daughter destined to rule)* would nurse children? For I have borne him a son in his old age." ⁸The child grew, and was weaned. Abraham*(Father of nations)* made a great feast on the day that Isaac*(Laughter)* was weaned. ⁹Sarah*(Daughter destined to rule)* saw the son of Hagar*(Fugitive)* the Egyptian*(Much anxious one)*, whom she had borne to Abraham*(Father of nations)*, mocking. ¹⁰Therefore she said to Abraham*(Father of nations)*, "Cast out this servant and her son! For the son of this servant will not be heir with my son, Isaac*(Laughter)*." ¹¹The thing was very grievous in the sight of Abraham*(Father of nations)* on account of his son. ¹²Our God said to Abraham*(Father of nations)*, "Do not let it be grievous in your sight because of the boy, and because of your servant. In all that Sarah*(Daughter destined to rule)* says to you, listen to her voice. For your offspring will be accounted as from Isaac*(Laughter)*. ¹³I will also make a nation of the son of the servant, because he is your child." ¹⁴Abraham*(Father of nations)* rose up early in the morning, and took bread and a bottle of water, and gave it to Hagar*(Fugitive)*, putting it on her shoulder; and gave her the child, and sent her away. She departed, and wandered in the wilderness of Beersheba*(Well of promise)*. ¹⁵The water in the bottle was spent, and she cast the child under one of the

shrubs. ¹⁶She went and sat down opposite him, a good way off, about a bow shot away. For she said, "Do not let me see the death of the child." She sat over against him, and lifted up her voice, and wept. ¹⁷Our God heard the voice of the boy. The angel of our God called to Hagar(*Fugitive*) out of the sky, and said to her, "What ails you, Hagar(*Fugitive*)? Do not be afraid. For our God has heard the voice of the boy where he is. ¹⁸Get up, lift up the boy, and hold him in your hand. For I will make him a great nation." ¹⁹Our God opened her eyes, and she saw a well of water. She went, filled the bottle with water, and gave the boy drink. ²⁰Our God was with the boy, and he grew. He lived in the wilderness, and became, as he grew up, an archer. ²¹He lived in the wilderness of Paran(*Glorious*). His mother took a wife for him out of the land of Egypt(*Double anxiety*). ²²At that time, Abimelech(*My father is king*) and Phicol(*Mouth of all*) the captain of his army spoke to Abraham(*Father of nations*), saying, "Our God is with you in all that you do. ²³Now, therefore, swear to me here by our God that you will not deal falsely with me, nor with my son, nor with my son's son. But according to the kindness that I have done to you, you will do to me, and to the land in which you have lived as a foreigner." ²⁴Abraham(*Father of nations*) said, "I will swear." ²⁵Abraham(*Father of nations*) complained to Abimelech(*My father is king*) because of a water well, which servants of Abimelech(*My father is king*) had violently taken away. ²⁶Abimelech(*My father is king*) said, "I do not know who has done this thing. You did not tell me, and I did not hear of it until today." ²⁷Abraham(*Father of nations*) took sheep and cattle, and gave them to Abimelech(*My father is king*). Those two made a covenant. ²⁸Abraham(*Father of nations*) set seven ewe lambs of the flock by themselves. ²⁹Abimelech(*My father is king*) said to Abraham(*Father of nations*), "What do these seven ewe lambs which you have set by themselves mean?" ³⁰He said, "You will take these seven ewe lambs from my hand, that it may be a witness to me, that I have dug this well." ³¹Therefore he called that place Beersheba(*Well of promise*), because they both swore there. ³²So they made a covenant at Beersheba(*Well of promise*). Abimelech(*My father is king*) rose up with Phicol(*Mouth of all*), the captain of his army, and they returned into the land of the Philistines(*Bringers of grief*). ³³Abraham(*Father of nations*) planted a tamarisk tree in Beersheba(*Well of promise*), and called there on the name of Yahweh(*Jealous one*) the Everlasting God. ³⁴Abraham(*Father of nations*) lived as a foreigner in the land of the Philistines(*Bringers *of grief*) many days.

CHAPTER 22

¹After these things, our God tested Abraham(*Father of nations*), and said to him, "Abraham(*Father of nations*)!" He said, "Here I am." ²He said, "Now take your son, your only son, whom you love, even Isaac(*Laughter*), and go into the land of Moriah(*Bitterness of Yahweh*). Offer him there as a burnt offering on one of the mountains which I will tell you of." ³Abraham(*Father of nations*) rose early in the morning, and saddled his donkey, and took two of his young men with him, and Isaac(*Laughter*) his son. He split the wood for the burnt offering, and rose up, and went to the place of which our God had told him. ⁴On the third day Abraham(*Father of nations*) lifted up his eyes, and saw the place far off. ⁵Abraham(*Father of nations*) said to his young men, "Stay here with the donkey. The boy and I will go yonder. We will worship, and come back to you." ⁶Abraham(*Father of nations*) took the wood of the burnt offering and laid it on Isaac(*Laughter*) his son. He took in his hand the fire and the knife. They both went together. ⁷Isaac(*Laughter*) spoke to Abraham(*Father of nations*) his father, and said, "My father?" He said, "Here I am, my son." He said, "Here is the fire and the wood, but where is the lamb for a burnt offering?" ⁸Abraham(*Father of nations*) said, "Our God will provide himself the lamb for a burnt offering, my son." So they both went together. ⁹They came to the place which our God had told him of. Abraham(*Father of nations*) built the altar there, and laid the wood in order, bound Isaac(*Laughter*) his son, and laid him on the altar, on the wood. ¹⁰Abraham(*Father of nations*) stretched out his hand, and took the knife to kill his son. ¹¹Angel-Yahweh(*Messenger of the Jealous one*) called to him out of the sky, and said, "Abraham(*Father of nations*), Abraham(*Father of nations*)!" He said, "Here I am." ¹²He said, "Do not lay your hand on the boy or do anything to him. For now I know that you fear our God, since you have not withheld your son, your only son, from me." ¹³Abraham(*Father of nations*) lifted up his eyes, and looked, and saw that behind him was a ram caught in the thicket by his horns. Abraham(*Father of nations*) went and took the ram, and offered him up for a

burnt offering instead of his son. ¹⁴Abraham(*Father of nations*) called the name of that place Yahweh(*Jealous one*) Will Provide. As it is said to this day, "On the mountain of Yahweh(*Jealous one*) it will be provided." ¹⁵Angel-Yahweh(*Messenger of the Jealous one*)) called to Abraham(*Father of nations*) a second time out of the sky, ¹⁶and said, "I have sworn by myself, says Yahweh(*Jealous one*), because you have done this thing, and have not withheld your son, your only son, ¹⁷that I will bless you greatly, and I will multiply your offspring greatly like the stars of the heavens, and like the sand which is on the seashore. Your offspring will possess the gate of his enemies. ¹⁸All the nations of the earth will be blessed by your offspring, because you have obeyed my voice." ¹⁹So Abraham(*Father of nations*) returned to his young men, and they rose up and went together to Beersheba(*Well of promise*). Abraham(*Father of nations*) lived at Beersheba(*Well of promise*). ²⁰After these things, Abraham(*Father of nations*) was told, "Behold, Milcah(*Queen*), she also has borne children to your brother Nahor(*Snorting*): ²¹Uz(*Counsel*) his firstborn, Buz(*Contempt*) his brother, Kemuel(*Risen up by God*) the father of Aram(*Elevated*), ²²Chesed (*Astrologer*), Hazo(*Visionary*), Pildash(*Fiery iron*), Jidlaph(*He drips*), and Bethuel(*Dweller in God*)." ²³Bethuel(*Dweller in God*) became the father of Rebekah(*Securely bound*). These eight Milcah (*Queen*) bore to Nahor(*Snorting*), brother of Abraham(*Father of nations*). ²⁴His concubine, whose name was Reumah(*Exalted*), also gave birth to Tebah(*Butcher*), Gaham(*Sunburnt*), Tahash(*Hurrier*), and Maacah(*One who squeezes*).

CHAPTER 23

¹Sarah(*Daughter destined to rule*) lived one hundred twenty-seven years. This was the length of the life of Sarah(*Daughter destined to rule*). ²Sarah(*Daughter destined to rule*) died in Kiriath-Arba(*Foursquared walled city*) [also called Hebron(*Alliance*)], in the land of Canaan(*Brought low*). Abraham(*Father of nations*) came to mourn for Sarah(*Daughter destined to rule*), and to weep for her. ³Abraham(*Father of nations*) rose up from before his dead, and spoke to the children of Heth(*Exhausted*), saying, ⁴"I am a stranger and a foreigner living with you. Give me possession of a burying-place with you, that I may bury my dead out of my sight." ⁵The children of Heth(*Exhausted*) answered Abraham(*Father of nations*), saying to him, ⁶"Hear us, my lord. You are a prince of the God among us. Bury your dead in the best of our tombs. None of us will withhold from you his tomb. Bury your dead." ⁷Abraham(*Father of nations*) rose up, and bowed himself to the people of the land, even to the children of Heth(*Exhausted*). ⁸He talked with them, saying, "If you agree that I should bury my dead out of my sight, hear me, and entreat for me to Ephron(*Antelope*) the son of Zohar(*Whiteness*), ⁹that he may give me the cave of Machpelah(*One above another*), which he has, which is in the end of his field. For the full price let him give it to me among you for a possession of a burying-place." ¹⁰Now Ephron(*Antelope*) was sitting in the middle of the children of Heth(*Exhausted*). Ephron(*Antelope*) the Hittite(*Terrorist*) answered Abraham(*Father of nations*) in the hearing of the children of Heth(*Exhausted*), even of all who went in at the gate of his city, saying, ¹¹"No, my lord, hear me. I give you the field, and I give you the cave that is in it. In the presence of the children of my people I give it to you. Bury your dead." ¹²Abraham(*Father of nations*) bowed himself down before the people of the land. ¹³He spoke to Ephron(*Antelope*) in the audience of the people of the land, saying, "But if you will, please hear me. I will give the price of the field. Take it from me, and I will bury my dead there." ¹⁴Ephron(*Antelope*) answered Abraham (*Father of nations*), saying to him, ¹⁵"My lord, listen to me. What is a piece of land worth four hun-

dred shekels of silver between me and you? Therefore bury your dead." ¹⁶Abraham (*Father of nations*) listened to Ephron(*Antelope*). Abraham (*Father of nations*) weighed to Ephron(*Antelope*) the silver which he had named in the audience of the children of Heth(*Exhausted*), four hundred shekels of silver, according to the current merchants' standard. ¹⁷So the field of Ephron(*Antelope*), which was in Machpelah(*One above another*), which was before Mamre(*Revealed from seeing*), the field, the cave which was in it, and all the trees that were in the field, that were in all of its borders, were deeded ¹⁸to Abraham(*Father of nations*) for a possession in the presence of the children of Heth(*Exhausted*), before all who went in at the gate of his city. ¹⁹After this, Abraham(*Father of nations*) buried Sarah(*Daughter destined to rule*) his wife in the cave of the field of Machpelah(*One above another*) before Mamre(*Revealed from seeing*) [that is, Hebron(*Alliance*)], in the land of Canaan(*Brought low*). ²⁰The field, and the cave that is in it, were deeded to Abraham(*Father of nations*) for possession of a burying place by the children of Heth(*Exhausted*).

CHAPTER 24

¹Abraham(*Father of nations*) was old, and well advanced in age. Yahweh(*Jealous one*) had blessed Abraham(*Father of nations*) in all things. ²Abraham(*Father of nations*) said to his servant, the elder of his house, who ruled over all that he had, "Please put your hand under my thigh. ³I will make you swear by Yahweh(*Jealous one*), the God of heaven and the God of the earth, that you will not take a wife for my son of the daughters of the Canaanites(*Ones brought low*), among whom I live. ⁴But you will go to my country, and to my relatives, and take a wife for my son Isaac(*Laughter*)." ⁵The servant said to him, "What if the woman is not willing to follow me to this land? Must I bring your son again to the land you came from?" ⁶Abraham(*Father of nations*) said to him, "Beware that you do not bring my son there again. ⁷Yahweh(*Jealous one*) the God of heaven, who took me from my father's house, and from the land of my birth, who spoke to me, and who swore to me, saying, 'I will give this land to your offspring. He will send his angel before you, and you will take a wife for my son from there. ⁸If the woman is not willing to follow you, then you will be clear from this promise to me. Only you will not bring my son there again." ⁹The servant put his hand under the thigh of Abraham(*Father of nations*) his master, and swore to him concerning this matter. ¹⁰The servant took ten camels, of his master's camels, and departed, having a variety of good things of his master's with him. He arose, and went to Mesopotamia(*Between two rivers*), to the city of Nahor(*Snorting*). ¹¹He made the camels kneel down outside the city by the well of water at the time of evening, the time that women go out to draw water. ¹²He said, "Yahweh(*Jealous one*), the God of my master Abraham(*Father of nations*), please give me success today, and show kindness to my master Abraham(*Father of nations*). ¹³Behold, I am standing by the spring of water. The daughters of the men of the city are coming out to draw water. ¹⁴Let it happen, that the young lady to whom I will say, 'Please let down your pitcher, that I may drink,' and she will say, 'Drink, and I will also give your camels a drink,'—let her be the one you

have appointed for your servant Isaac(*Laughter*). By this I will know that you have shown kindness to my master." **15**Before he had finished speaking, behold, Rebekah(*Securely bound*) came out, who was born to Bethuel (*Dweller in God*) the son of Milcah(*Queen*), the wife of Nahor(*Snorting*), brother of Abraham(*Father of nations*), with her pitcher on her shoulder. **16**The young lady was very beautiful to look at, a virgin. No man had known her. She went down to the spring, filled her pitcher, and came up. **17**The servant ran to meet her, and said, "Please give me a drink, a little water from your pitcher." **18**She said, "Drink, my lord." She hurried, and let down her pitcher on her hand, and gave him drink. **19**When she had done giving him drink, she said, "I will also draw for your camels, until they have done drinking." **20**She hurried, and emptied her pitcher into the trough, and ran again to the well to draw, and drew for all his camels. **21**The man looked steadfastly at her, remaining silent, to know whether Yahweh(*Jealous one*) had made his journey prosperous or not. **22**As the camels had done drinking, the man took a golden ring of half a shekels weight, and two bracelets for her hands of ten shekels weight of gold, **23**and said, "Whose daughter are you? Please tell me. Is there room in your father's house for us to lodge in?" **24**She said to him, "I am the daughter of Bethuel(*Dweller in God*) the son of Milcah(*Queen*), whom she bore to Nahor(*Snorting*)." **25**She said moreover to him, "We have both straw and feed enough, and room to lodge in." **26**The man bowed his head, and worshiped Yahweh(*Jealous one*). **27**He said, "Blessed be Yahweh(*Jealous one*) the God of my master Abraham(*Father of nations*), who has not forsaken his loving kindness and his truth toward my master. As for me, Yahweh(*Jealous one*) has led me on the way to the house of my master's relatives." **28**The young lady ran, and told her mother's house about these words. **29**Rebekah had a brother, and his name was Laban(*White*). Laban(*White*) ran out to the man, to the spring. **30**When he saw the ring, and the bracelets on his sister's hands, and when he heard the words of Rebekah(*Securely bound*) his sister, saying, "This is what the man said to me," he came to the man. Behold, he was standing by the camels at the spring. **31**He said, "Come in, you blessed of Yahweh(*Jealous one*). Why do you stand outside? For I have prepared the house, and room for the camels." **32**The man came into the house, and he unloaded the camels. He gave straw and feed for the camels, and water to wash his feet and the feet of the men who were with him. **33**Food was set before him to eat, but he said, "I will not eat until I have told my message." He said, "Speak on." ³⁴He said, "I am the servant of Abraham(*Father of nations*). ³⁵Yahweh(*Jealous one*) has blessed my master greatly. He has become great. He has given him flocks and herds, silver and gold, male servants and female servants, and camels and donkeys. ³⁶Sarah(*Daughter destined to rule*), my master's wife, bore a son to my master when she was old. He has given all that he has to him. ³⁷My master made me swear, saying, 'You will not take a wife for my son from the daughters of the Canaanites(*Ones brought low*), in whose land I live, ³⁸but you will go to my father's house, and to my relatives, and take a wife for my son.' ³⁹I asked my master, 'What if the woman will not follow me?' ⁴⁰He said to me, 'Yahweh(*Jealous one*), before whom I walk, will send his angel with you, and prosper your way. You will take a wife for my son from my relatives, and of my father's house. ⁴¹Then will you be clear from my promise, when you come to my relatives. If they do not give her to you, you will be clear from my promise.' ⁴² I came today to the spring, and said, 'Yahweh(*Jealous one*) the God of my master Abraham(*Father of nations*), if now you do prosper my way which I go — ⁴³behold, I am standing by this spring of water. Let it happen, that the maiden who comes out to draw, to whom I will say, "Please give me a little water from your pitcher to drink," ⁴⁴and she will tell me, "Drink, and I will also draw for your camels,"—let her be the woman whom Yahweh(*Jealous one*) has appointed for my master's son.' ⁴⁵Before I had finished speaking in my heart, behold, Rebekah(*Securely bound*) came out with her pitcher on her shoulder. She went down to the spring, and drew. I said to her, 'Please let me drink.' ⁴⁶She hurried and let down her pitcher from her shoulder, and said, 'Drink, and I will also give your camels a drink.' So I drank, and she also gave the camels a drink. ⁴⁷I asked her, and said, 'Whose daughter are you?' She said, 'The daughter of Bethuel(*Dweller in God*), son of Nahor(*Snorting*), whom Milcah(*Queen*) bore to him.' I put the ring on her nose, and the bracelets on her hands. ⁴⁸I bowed my head, and worshiped Yahweh(*Jealous one*), and blessed Yahweh(*Jealous one*), the God of my master Abraham(*Father of nations*), who had led me in the right way to take my master's brother's daughter for his son. ⁴⁹Now if you will deal kindly and truly with my master, tell me. If not, tell me, that I may turn to the right hand, or to the left." ⁵⁰Then Laban(*White*) and Bethuel(*Dweller in God*) answered, "The thing proceeds from Yahweh(*Jealous one*). We cannot speak to you bad or good. ⁵¹Behold, Rebekah(*Securely bound*) is before you. Take her, and go, and let her be your master's son's wife, as Yahweh(*Jealous one*) has spoken." ⁵²When the servant of Abraham(*Father of nations*) servant heard their words, he bowed himself down to the earth to Yahweh(*Jealous one*). ⁵³The servant brought out jewels of silver, and jewels of gold, and clothing, and gave them to Rebekah(*Securely bound*). He also gave precious things to her brother and her mother. ⁵⁴They ate and drank, he and the men who were with him, and stayed all night. They rose up in the morning, and he said, "Send me away to my master." ⁵⁵Her brother and her mother said, "Let the young lady stay with us a few days, at least ten. After that she will go." ⁵⁶ He said to them, "Do not hinder me, since Yahweh(*Jealous one*) has prospered my way. Send me away that I may go to my master." ⁵⁷They said, "We will call the young lady, and ask her." ⁵⁸They called Rebekah(*Securely bound*), and said to her, "Will you go with this man?" She said, "I will go." ⁵⁹They sent away Rebekah(*Securely bound*), their sister, with her nurse, the servant of Abraham(*Father of nations*), and his men. ⁶⁰They blessed Rebekah(*Securely bound*), and said to her, "Our sister, may you be the mother of thousands of ten thousands, and let your offspringt possess the gate of those who hate them." ⁶¹Rebekah arose with her ladies. They rode on the camels, and followed the man. The servant took Rebekah(*Securely bound*), and went his way. ⁶²Isaac(*Laughter*) came from the way of Beer-Lahai-Roi(*A well of vision for life*), for he lived in the land of the Negev(*South*). ⁶³Isaac(*Laughter*) went out to meditate in the field at the evening. He lifted up his eyes, and saw, and, behold, there were camels coming. ⁶⁴Rebekah lifted up her eyes, and when she saw Isaac(*Laughter*), she dismounted from the camel. ⁶⁵She said to the servant, "Who is the man who is walking in the field to meet us?" The servant said, "It is my master." She took her veil, and covered herself. ⁶⁶The servant told Isaac(*Laughter*) all the things that he had done. ⁶⁷Isaac(*Laughter*) brought her into the tent of his mother Sarah(*Daughter destined to rule*), and took Rebekah(*Securely bound*), and she became his wife. He loved her. Isaac(*Laughter*) was comforted after his mother's death.

CHAPTER 25

¹Abraham(*Father of nations*) took another wife, and her name was Keturah(*Incense*). ²She bore to him Zimran(*One who prunes*), Jokshan(*One who traps*), Medan(*Judgment*), Midian(*Strife*), Ishbak(*He will let go*), and Shuah(*Depression*). ³Jokshan became the father of Sheba(*Sworn promise*), and Dedan(*Moving forward*). The sons of Dedan(*Moving forward*) were Asshurim(*Stepping forward*), Letushim(*Metal workers*), and Leummim(*Peoples*). ⁴The sons of Midian(*Strife*) were: Ephah(*Darkness*), Epher(*Dust*), Hanoch(*Dedicate*), Abida(*My father knows*), and Eldaah(*God called*) . All these were the children of Keturah(*Incense*). ⁵Abraham (*Father of nations*) gave all that he had to Isaac(*Laughter*), ⁶but to the sons of the concubines of Abraham(*Father of nations*) he gave gifts. Abraham(*Father of nations*) sent them away from Isaac(*Laughter*) his son, while he yet lived, eastward, to the east country. ⁷These are the days of the years of the life of Abraham(*Father of nations*) which he lived: one hundred seventy-five years. ⁸Abraham(*Father of nations*) gave up his spirit, and died in a good old age, an old man, and full of years, and was gathered to his people. ⁹Isaac(*Laughter*) and Ishmael(*God listens*), his sons, buried him in the cave of Machpelah(*One above another*), in the field of Ephron(*Antelope*), the son of Zohar(*Whiteness*) the Hittite(*Terrorist*), which is before Mamre(*Revealed from seeing*), ¹⁰the field which Abraham(*Father of nations*) purchased of the children of Heth(*Exhausted*). Abraham(*Father of nations*) was buried there with Sarah(*Daughter destined to rule*), his wife. ¹¹After the death of Abraham(*Father of nations*), our God blessed Isaac(*Laughter*), his son. Isaac(*Laughter*) lived by Beer-Lahai-Roi(*A well of vision for life*). ¹²Now this is the history of the generations of Ishmael(*God listens*), the son of Abraham(*Father of nations*), whom Hagar(*Fugitive*) the Egyptian(*Much anxious one*), servant of Sarah(*Daughter destined to rule*), bore to Abraham(*Father of nations*). ¹³These are the names of the sons of Ishmael(*God listens*), by their names, according to the order of their birth: the firstborn of Ishmael(*God listens*), Nebaioth(*Prophecies*), then Kedar(*Dark one*), Adbeel(*Sorrow of God*), Mib-

sam(*Pleasant smelling*), ¹⁴Mishma(*Rumor*), Dumah(*Silence*), Massa(*Burden*), ¹⁵Hadad(*Sharpened*), Tema(*Southerner*), Jetur(*He will establish borders*), Naphish(*Refreshed soul*), and Kedemah (*Eastward*). ¹⁶These are the sons of Ishmael(*God listens*), and these are their names, by their villages, and by their encampments: twelve princes, according to their nations. ¹⁷These are the years of the life of Ishmael(*God listens*): one hundred thirty-seven years. He gave up his spirit and died, and was gathered to his people. ¹⁸They lived from Havilah(*Birthing*) to Shur(*Raised wall*) that is before Egypt(*Double anxiety*), as you go toward Assyria(*Stepping forward*). He lived opposite all his relatives. ¹⁹This is the history of the generations of Isaac(*Laughter*), son of Abraham(*Father of nations*). Abraham(*Father of nations*) became the father of Isaac(*Laughter*). ²⁰Isaac(*Laughter*) was forty years old when he took Rebekah(*Securely bound*), the daughter of Bethuel(*Dweller in God*) the Syrian(*Elevated one*) of Paddan-Aram(*Elevated plane*), the sister of Laban(*White*) the Syrian(*Elevated one*), to be his wife. ²¹Isaac(*Laughter*) boldy petitioned Yahweh(*Jealous one*) for his wife, because she was barren. Yahweh(*Jealous one*) was boldy petitioned by him, and Rebekah(*Securely bound*) his wife conceived. ²²The children struggled together within her. She said, "If it is so, why do I live?" She went to inquire of Yahweh(*Jealous one*). ²³Yahweh(*Jealous one*) said to her, "Two nations are in your womb. Two peoples will be separated from your body. The one people will be stronger than the other people. The elder will serve the younger." ²⁴When her days to be delivered were fulfilled, behold, there were twins in her womb. ²⁵The first came out red all over, like a hairy garment. They named him Esau(*Hairy*). ²⁶After that, his brother came out, and his hand had hold on the heel of Esau(*Hairy*). He was named Jacob(*Heel grabber*). Isaac(*Laughter*) was sixty years old when she gave birth to them. ²⁷The boys grew. Esau(*Hairy*) was a skillful hunter, a man of the field. Jacob(*Heel grabber*) was a quiet man, living in tents. ²⁸Now Isaac(*Laughter*) loved Esau(*Hairy*), because he ate his venison. Rebekah(*Securely bound*) loved Jacob(*Heel grabber*). ²⁹Jacob (*Heel grabber*) boiled stew. Esau(*Hairy*) came in from the field, and he was famished. ³⁰Esau(*Hairy*) said to Jacob(*Heel grabber*), "Please feed me with that same red stew, for I am famished." Therefore his name was called Edom(*Red*). ³¹Jacob(*Heel grabber*) said, "First, sell me your birthright." ³²Esau(*Hairy*) said, "Behold, I am about to die. What good is the birthright to me?" ³³Jacob(*Heel grabber*) said, "Swear to me first." He swore to him. He sold his birthright to Jacob(*Heel grabber*). ³⁴Jacob(*Heel grabber*) gave Esau(*Hairy*) bread and stew of lentils. He ate and drank, rose up, and went his way. So Esau(*Hairy*) despised his birthright.

CHAPTER 26

¹There was a famine in the land, besides the first famine that was in the days of Abraham(*Father of nations*). Isaac(*Laughter*) went to Abimelech(*My Father is king*) king of the Philistines(*Bringers of grief*), to Gerar(*Dragged away*). ²Yahweh(*Jealous one*) appeared to him, and said, "Do not go down into Egypt(*Double anxiety*). Live in the land I will tell you about. ³Live in this land, and I will be with you, and will bless you. For I will give to you, and to your offspring, all these lands, and I will establish the promise which I swore to Abraham(*Father of nations*) your father. ⁴I will multiply your offspring as the stars of the sky, and will give all these lands to your offspring. In your offspring will all the nations of the earth be blessed, ⁵because Abraham(*Father of nations*) obeyed my voice, and kept my requirements, my commandments, my statutes, and my laws." ⁶Isaac(*Laughter*) lived in Gerar(*Dragged away*). ⁷The men of the place asked him about his wife. He said, "She is my sister," for he was afraid to say, "My wife", unless, he thought, "the men of the place might kill me for Rebekah(*Securely bound*), because she is beautiful to look at." ⁸When he had been there a long time, Abimelech(*My Father is king*) king of the Philistines(*Bringers of grief*) looked out at a window, and saw, and, behold, Isaac(*Laughter*) was caressing Rebekah(*Securely bound*), his wife. ⁹Abimelech(*My father is king*) called Isaac(*Laughter*), and said, "Behold, surely she is your wife. Why did you say, 'She is my sister?'" Isaac(*Laughter*) said to him, "Because I said, 'Lest I die because of her.'" ¹⁰Abimelech(*My father is king*) said, "What is this you have done to us? One of the people might easily have lain with your wife, and you would have brought guilt on us!" ¹¹Abimelech(*My father is king*) commanded all the people, saying, "He who touches this man or his wife will surely be put to death." ¹²Isaac(*Laughter*) sowed in that land, and reaped in the same year one hundred times what he planted. Yahweh(*Jealous one*) blessed him. ¹³The man grew great, and grew more and more until he became very great. ¹⁴He had possessions of flocks, possessions of herds, and a great household. The Philistines(

Bringers of grief) envied him. **¹⁵**Now all the wells which his father's servants had dug in the days of Abraham(*Father of nations*) his father, the Philistines(*Bringers of grief*) had stopped, and filled with earth. **¹⁶**Abimelech(*My Father is king*) said to Isaac(*Laughter*), "Go from us, for you are much mightier than we." **¹⁷**Isaac(*Laughter*) departed from there, encamped in the valley of Gerar(*Dragged away*), and lived there. **¹⁸**Isaac(*Laughter*) dug again the wells of water, which they had dug in the days of Abraham(*Father of nations*) his father. For the Philistines(*Bringers of grief*) had stopped them after the death of Abraham(*Father of nations*). He called their names after the names by which his father had called them. **¹⁹**The servants of Isaac(*Laughter)* dug in the valley, and found there a well of springing water. **²⁰**The herdsmen of Gerar(*Dragged away*) argued with the herdsmen of Isaac(*Laughter*), saying, "The water is ours." He called the name of the well Esek(*Dispute*), because they contended with him. **²¹**They dug another well, and they argued over that, also. He called its name Sitnah(*Cease and desist order*). **²²**He left that place, and dug another well. They did not argue over that one. He called it Rehoboth(*Spacious*). He said, "For now Yahweh(*Jealous one*) has made room for us, and we will be fruitful in the land." **²³**He went up from there to Beersheba(*Well of promise*). **²⁴**Yahweh(*Jealous one*) appeared to him the same night, and said, "I am the God of Abraham(*Father of nations*) your father. Do not be afraid, for I am with you, and will bless you, and multiply your offspring for the sake of my servant Abraham(*Father of nations*)." **²⁵**He built an altar there, and called on the name of Yahweh(*Jealous one*), and pitched his tent there. There the servants of Isaac(*Laughter*) dug a well. **²⁶**Then Abimelech(*My father is king*) went to him from Gerar(*Dragged away*), and Ahuzzath(*Possession*) his friend, and Phicol(*Mouth of all*) the captain of his army. **²⁷**Isaac(*Laughter*) said to them, "Why have you come to me, since you hate me, and have sent me away from you?" **²⁸**They said, "We saw plainly that Yahweh(*Jealous one)* was with you. We said, 'Let there now be an promise between us, even between us and you, and let us make a covenant with you, **²⁹**that you will do us no harm, as we have not touched you, and as we have done to you nothing but good, and have sent you away in peace.' You are now the blessed of Yahweh(*Jealous one*)." **³⁰**He made them a feast, and they ate and drank. **³¹**They rose up some time in the morning, and swore a promise to one another. Isaac(*Laughter*) sent them away, and they departed from   him in peace. **³²**The same day, the servants of Isaac(*Laughter*) came, and told him concerning the well which they had dug, and said to him, "We have found water." ³³He called it Shibah(*Abundance*). Therefore the name of the city is Beersheba(*Well of oath*) to this day. ³⁴When Esau(*Hairy*) was forty years old, he took as wife Judith(*Praised)*, the daughter of Beeri(*My well*) the Hittite(*Terrorist*), and Basemath(*Perfumed*), the daughter of Elon (*Mighty oak*) the Hittite(*Terrorist*). ³⁵They grieved the spirits of Isaac(*Laughter*) and Rebekah(*Securely bound*).

CHAPTER 27

¹When Isaac(*Laughter*) was old, and his eyes were dim, so that he could not see, he called Esau(*Hairy*) his elder son, and said to him, "My son?" He said to him, "Here I am." ²He said, "See now, I am old. I do not know the day of my death. ³Now therefore, please take your weapons, your quiver and your bow, and go out to the field, and take me venison. ⁴Make me savory food, such as I love, and bring it to me, that I may eat, and that my soul may bless you before I die." ⁵Rebekah(*Securely bound*) heard when Isaac(*Laughter*) spoke to Esau(*Hairy*) his son. Esau(*Hairy*) went to the field to hunt for venison, and to bring it. ⁶Rebekah(*Securely bound*) spoke to Jacob(*Heel grabber*) her son, saying, "Behold, I heard your father speak to Esau(*Hairy*) your brother, saying, ⁷'Bring me venison, and make me savory food, that I may eat, and bless you before Yahweh(*Jealous one*) before my death.' ⁸Now therefore, my son, obey my voice according to that which I command you. ⁹Go now to the flock, and get me from there two good young goats. I will make them savory food for your father, such as he loves. ¹⁰You will bring it to your father, that he may eat, so that he may bless you before his death." ¹¹Jacob(*Heel grabber*) said to Rebekah(*Securely bound*) his mother, "Behold, Esau(*Hairy*) my brother is a hairy man, and I am a smooth man. ¹²What if my father touches me? I will seem to him as a deceiver, and I would bring a curse on myself, and not a blessing." ¹³His mother said to him, "Let your curse be on me, my son. Only obey my voice, and go get them for me." ¹⁴He went, and got them, and brought them to his mother. His mother made savory food, such as his father loved. ¹⁵Rebekah(*Securely bound*) took the good clothes of Esau(*Hairy*), her elder son, which were with her in the house, and put them on Jacob(*Heel grabber*), her younger son. ¹⁶She put the skins of the young goats on his hands, and on the smooth of his neck. ¹⁷She gave the savory food and the bread, which she had prepared, into the hand of her son Jacob(*Heel grabber*). ¹⁸He came to his father, and said, "My father?" He said, "Here I am. Who are you, my son?" ¹⁹Jacob(*Heel grabber*) said to his father, "I am Esau(*Hairy*) your

firstborn. I have done what you asked me to do. Please arise, sit and eat of my venison, that your soul may bless me." ²⁰Isaac(*Laughter*) said to his son, "How is it that you have found it so quickly, my son?" He said, "Because Yahweh(*Jealous one*) our God gave me success." ²¹Isaac(*Laughter*) said to Jacob(*Heel grabber*), "Please come near, that I may feel you, my son, whether you are really my son Esau(*Hairy*) or not." ²²Jacob(*Heel grabber*) went near to Isaac(*Laughter*) his father. He felt him, and said, "The voice is the voice of Jacob(*Heel grabber*), but the hands are the hands of Esau(*Hairy*)." ²³He did not recognize him, because his hands were hairy, like his brother, the hands of Esau(*Hairy*). So he blessed him. ²⁴He said, "Are you really my son Esau(*Hairy*)?" He said, "I am." ²⁵He said, "Bring it near to me, and I will eat of my son's venison, that my soul may bless you." He brought it near to him, and he ate. He brought him wine, and he drank. ²⁶His father Isaac(*Laughter*) said to him, "Come near now, and kiss me, my son." ²⁷He came near, and kissed him. He smelled the smell of his clothing, and blessed him, and said, "Behold, the smell of my son is as the smell of a field which Yahweh(*Jealous one*) has blessed. ²⁸May our God give you of the dew of the sky, of the fatness of the earth, and plenty of grain and new wine. ²⁹Let peoples serve you, and nations bow down to you. Be lord over your brothers. Let your mother's sons bow down to you. Cursed be everyone who curses you. Blessed be everyone who blesses you." ³⁰As soon as Isaac(*Laughter*) had finished blessing Jacob(*Heel grabber*), and Jacob(*Heel grabber*) had just gone out from the presence of Isaac(*Laughter*) his father, Esau(*Hairy*) his brother came in from his hunting. ³¹He also made savory food, and brought it to his father. He said to his father, "Let my father arise, and eat of his son's venison, that your soul may bless me." ³²Isaac(*Laughter*) his father said to him, "Who are you?" He said, "I am your son, your firstborn, Esau(*Hairy*)." ³³Isaac(*Laughter*) trembled violently, and said, "Who, then, is he who has taken venison, and brought it me, and I have eaten of all before you came, and have blessed him? Yes, he will be blessed." ³⁴When Esau(*Hairy*) heard the words of his father, he cried with an exceeding great and bitter cry, and said to his father, "Bless me, even me also, my father." ³⁵He said, "Your brother came with deceit, and has taken away your blessing." ³⁶He said, "Is not he rightly named Jacob(*Heel grabber*)? For he has supplanted me these two times. He took away my birthright. See, now he has taken away my blessing." He said, "Have not you reserved a blessing for me?" ³⁷Isaac(*Laughter*) answered Esau(*Hairy*), "Behold, I have made him your lord, and all his brothers have I given to him for servants. With grain and new wine have I sustained him. What then will I do for you, my son?" ³⁸Esau(*Hairy*) said to his father, "Have you but one blessing, my father? Bless me, even me also, my father." Esau(*Hairy*) lifted up his voice, and wept. ³⁹Isaac(*Laughter*) his father answered him, "Behold, of the fatness of the earth will be your dwelling, and of the dew of the sky from above. ⁴⁰By your sword will you live, and you will serve your brother. It will happen, when you will break loose, that you will shake his yoke from off your neck." ⁴¹Esau(*Hairy*) hated Jacob(*Heel grabber*) because of the blessing with which his father blessed him. Esau(*Hairy*) said in his heart, "The days of mourning for my father are at hand. Then I will kill my brother Jacob(*Heel grabber*)." ⁴²The words of Esau(*Hairy*), her elder son, were told to Rebekah(*Securely bound*). She sent and called Jacob(*Heel grabber*), her younger son, and said to him, "Behold, your brother Esau(*Hairy*) comforts himself about you by planning to kill you. ⁴³Now therefore, my son, obey my voice. Arise, flee to Laban(*White*), my brother, in Haran(*Dry place*). ⁴⁴Stay with him a few days, until your brother's fury turns away; ⁴⁵until your brother's anger turn away from you, and he forgets what you have done to him. Then I will send, and get you from there. Why should I be bereaved of you both in one day?" ⁴⁶Rebekah (*Securely bound*) said to Isaac(*Laughter*), "I am weary of my life because of the daughters of Heth(*Exhausted*). If Jacob(*Heel grabber*) takes a wife of the daughters of Heth(*Exhausted*), such as these, of the daughters of the land, what good will my life do me?"

CHAPTER 28

¹Isaac(*Laughter*) called Jacob(*Heel grabber*), blessed him, and commanded him, "You will not take a wife of the daughters of Canaan(*Brought low*). ²Arise, go to Paddan-Aram(*Elevated plain*), to the house of Bethuel(*Dweller in God*) your mother's father. Take a wife from there from the daughters of Laban(*White*), your mother's brother. ³May the God who is enough bless you, and make you fruitful, and multiply you, that you may be a company of peoples, ⁴and give you the blessing of Abraham(*Father of nations*), to you, and to your offspring with you, that you may inherit the land where you travel, which God gave to Abraham(*Father of nations*)." ⁵Isaac (*Laughter*) sent Jacob(*Heel grabber*) away. He went to Paddan-Aram(*Elevated plain*) to Laban(*White*), son of Bethuel(*Dweller in God*) the Syrian(*Elevated one*), the brother of Rebekah(*Securely bound*), the mother of Jacob(*Heel grabber*) and Esau(*Hairy*). ⁶Now Esau(*Hairy*) saw that Isaac(*Laughter*) had blessed Jacob(*Heel grabber*) and sent him away to Paddan-Aram(*Elevated plain*), to take him a wife from there, and that as he blessed him he gave him a command, saying, "You will not take a wife of the daughters of Canaan(*Brought low*)," ⁷and that Jacob(*Heel grabber*) obeyed his father and his mother, and was gone to Paddan-Aram(*Elevated plain*). ⁸Esau(*Hairy*) saw that the daughters of Canaan(*Brought low*) did not please Isaac(*Laughter*), his father. ⁹Esau(*Hairy*) went to Ishmael(*God listens*), and took, besides the wives that he had, Mahalath(*Sad song*) the daughter of Ishmael(*God listens*), the son of Abraham(*Father of nations*), the sister of Nebaioth(*Prophecies*), to be his wife. ¹⁰Jacob(*Heel grabber*) went out from Beersheba(*Well of promise),* and went toward Haran(*Dry place*). ¹¹He came to a certain place, and stayed there all night, because the sun had set. He took one of the stones of the place, and put it under his head, and lay down in that place to sleep. ¹²He dreamed. Behold, a stairway set upon the earth, and its top reached to heaven. Behold, the angels of God ascending and descending on it. ¹³Behold, Yahweh(*Jealous one*) stood above it, and said, "I am Yahweh(*Jealous one*), the God of Abraham(*Father of nations*) your father, and the

God of Isaac(*Laughter*). The land whereon you lie, to you will I give it, and to your offspring. ¹⁴Your offspring will be as the dust of the earth, and you will spread abroad to the west, and to the east, and to the north, and to the south. In you and in your offspring will all the families of the earth be blessed. ¹⁵Behold, I am with you, and will keep you, wherever you go, and will bring you again into this land. For I will not leave you, until I have done that which I have spoken of to you." ¹⁶Jacob(*Heel grabber*) awakened out of his sleep, and he said, "Surely Yahweh(*Jealous one*) is in this place, and I did not know it." ¹⁷He was afraid, and said, "How dreadful is this place! This is none other than the house of our God, and this is the gate of heaven." ¹⁸Jacob(*Heel grabber*) rose up early in the morning, and took the stone that he had put under his head, and set it up for a pillar, and poured oil on its top. ¹⁹He called the name of that place Bethel(*House of God*), but the name of the city was Luz(*Almond tree*) at the first. ²⁰Jacob(*Heel grabber*) vowed a vow, saying, "If this God will be with me, and will keep me in this way that I go, and will give me bread to eat, and clothing to put on, ²¹so that I come again to my father's house in peace, and Yahweh(*Jealous one*) will be my God, ²²then this stone, which I have set up for a pillar, will be the house of my God. Of all that you will give me I will surely give a tenth to you."

CHAPTER 29

¹Then Jacob(*Heel grabber*) went on his journey, and came to the land of the children of the east. ²He looked, and behold, a well in the field, and, behold, three flocks of sheep lying there by it. For out of that well they watered the flocks. The stone on the well's mouth was large. ³There all the flocks were gathered. They rolled the stone from the well's mouth, and watered the sheep, and put the stone again on the well's mouth in its place. ⁴Jacob(*Heel grabber*) said to them, "My relatives, where are you from?" They said, "We are from Haran(*Dry place*)." ⁵He said to them, "Do you know Laban(*White*), the son of Nahor(*Snorting*)?" They said, "We know him." ⁶He said to them, "Is it well with him?" They said, "It is well. See, Rachel(*Lamb*), his daughter, is coming with the sheep." ⁷He said, "Behold, it is still the middle of the day, not time to gather the livestock together. Water the sheep, and go and feed them." ⁸They said, "We cannot, until all the flocks are gathered together, and they roll the stone from the well's mouth. Then we water the sheep." ⁹While he was yet speaking with them, Rachel(*Lamb*) came with her father's sheep, for she kept them. ¹⁰When Jacob(*Heel grabber*) saw Rachel(*Lamb*) the daughter of Laban(*White*), his mother's brother, and the sheep of Laban(*White*), his mother's brother, Jacob(*Heel grabber*) went near, and rolled the stone from the well's mouth, and watered the flock of Laban(*White*) his mother's brother. ¹¹Jacob(*Heel grabber*) kissed Rachel (*Lamb*), and lifted up his voice, and wept. ¹²Jacob(*Heel grabber*) told Rachel(*Lamb*) that he was her father's brother, and that he was the son of Rebekah(*Securely bound*). She ran and told her father. ¹³When Laban(*White*) heard the news of Jacob(*Heel grabber*), his sister's son, he ran to meet Jacob(*Heel grabber*), and embraced him, and kissed him, and brought him to his house. Jacob(*Heel grabber*) told Laban(*White*) all these things. ¹⁴Laban(*White*) said to him, "Surely you are my bone and my flesh." He lived with him for a month. ¹⁵Laban(*White*) said to Jacob(*Heel grabber*), "Because you are my brother, should you therefore serve me for nothing? Tell me, what will your wages be?" ¹⁶Laban(*White*) had two daughters. The name of

the elder was Leah(*Wearied*), and the name of the younger was Rachel(*Lamb*). ¹⁷The eyes of Leah(*Wearied*) were weak, but Rachel(*Lamb*) was beautiful in form and attractive. ¹⁸Jacob(*Heel grabber*) loved Rachel(*Lamb*). He said, "I will serve you seven years for Rachel(*Lamb*), your younger daughter." ¹⁹Laban(*White*) said, "It is better that I give her to you, than that I should give her to another man. Stay with me." ²⁰Jacob(*Heel grabber*) served seven years for Rachel(*Lamb*). They seemed to him but a few days, for the love he had for her. ²¹Jacob(*Heel grabber*) said to Laban(*White*), "Give me my wife, for my days are fulfilled, that I may go in to her." ²²Laban(*White*) gathered together all the men of the place, and made a feast. ²³In the evening, he took Leah(*Wearied*) his daughter, and brought her to him. He went in to her. ²⁴Laban(*White*) gave Zilpah(*A drop*) his servant to his daughter Leah(*Wearied*) for a servant. ²⁵In the morning, behold, it was Leah(*Wearied*). He said to Laban(*White*), "What is this you have done to me? Did not I serve with you for Rachel(*Lamb*)? Why then have you deceived me?" ²⁶Laban(*White*) said, "It is not done so in our place, to give the younger before the firstborn. ²⁷Fulfill the week of this one, and we will give you the other also for the service which you will serve with me yet seven other years." ²⁸Jacob(*Heel grabber*) did so, and fulfilled her week. He gave him Rachel(*Lamb*) his daughter as wife. ²⁹Laban(*White*) gave to Rachel(*Lamb*) his daughter Bilhah(*Troubled*), his servant, to be her servant. ³⁰He went in also to Rachel(*Lamb*), and he loved also Rachel(*Lamb*) more than Leah(*Wearied*), and served with him yet seven other years. ³¹Yahweh(*Jealous one*) saw that Leah(*Wearied*) was hated, and he opened her womb, but Rachel(*Lamb*) was barren. ³²Leah(*Wearied*) conceived, and gave birth to a son, and she named him Reuben(*I see a son!*). For she said, "Because Yahweh(*Jealous one*) has looked at my affliction. For now my husband will love me." ³³She conceived again, and gave birth to a son, and said, "Because Yahweh(*Jealous one*) has heard that I am hated, he has therefore given me this son also." She named him Simeon(*One who heard and obeyed*). ³⁴She conceived again, and gave birth to a son. Said, "Now this time will my husband be joined to me, because I have borne him three sons." Therefore his name was called Levi(*Attached*). ³⁵She conceived again, and gave birth to a son. She said, "This time will I praise Yahweh(*Jealous one*)." Therefore she named him Judah(*One who praises*). Then she stopped bearing.

CHAPTER 30

¹When Rachel(*Lamb*) saw that she bore Jacob(*Heel grabber*) no children, Rachel(*Lamb*) envied her sister. She said to Jacob(*Heel grabber*), "Give me children, or else I will die." ²The anger of Jacob(*Heel grabber*) burned against Rachel(*Lamb*), and he said, "Am I in place of our God, who has withheld from you the fruit of the womb?" ³She said, "Behold, my maid Bilhah(*Troubled*). Go in to her, that she may bear on my knees, and I also may obtain children by her." ⁴She gave him Bilhah(*Troubled*) her servant as wife, and Jacob(*Heel grabber*) went in to her. ⁵Bilhah(*Troubled*) conceived, and bore Jacob(*Heel grabber*) a son. ⁶Rachel(*Lamb*) said, "Our God has judged me, and has also heard my voice, and has given me a son." Therefore called she his name Dan(*One who judges*). ⁷Bilhah(*Troubled*), the servant of Rachel(*Lamb*), conceived again, and bore to Jacob(*Heel grabber*) a second son. ⁸Rachel(*Lamb*) said, "With mighty wrestlings have I wrestled with my sister, and have prevailed." She named him Naphtali(*My struggle*). ⁹When Leah(*Wearied*) saw that she had finished bearing, she took Zilpah(*A drop*), her servant, and gave her to Jacob(*Heel grabber*) as a wife. ¹⁰Zilpah, the servant of Leah(*Wearied*), bore to Jacob(*Heel grabber*) a son. ¹¹Leah(*Wearied*) said, "How fortunate!" She named him Gad(*Fortunate*). ¹²Zilpah, the servant of Leah(*Wearied*), bore to Jacob(*Heel grabber*) a second son. ¹³Leah(*Wearied*) said, "Happy am I, for the daughters will call me happy." She named him Asher(*Happy*). ¹⁴Reuben(*I see a son!*) went in the days of wheat harvest, and found mandrakes in the field, and brought them to his mother, Leah(*Wearied*). Then Rachel(*Lamb*) said to Leah(*Wearied*), "Please give me some of your son's mandrakes." ¹⁵She said to her, "Is it a small matter that you have taken away my husband? Would you take away my son's mandrakes, also?" Rachel(*Lamb*) said, "Therefore he will lie with you tonight for your son's mandrakes." ¹⁶Jacob(*Heel grabber*) came from the field in the evening, and Leah(*Wearied*) went out to meet him, and said, "You must come into me; for I have surely hired you with my son's mandrakes." He lay with her that night. ¹⁷Our God listened to Leah(*Wearied*), and she conceived,

and bore to Jacob(*Heel grabber*) a fifth son. ¹⁸Leah(*Wearied*) said, "Our God has given me my hire, because I gave my servant to my husband." She named him Issachar(*Hired for wage*). ¹⁹Leah(*Wearied*) conceived again, and bore a sixth son to Jacob(*Heel grabber*). ²⁰Leah(*Wearied*) said, "Our God has endowed me with a good dowry. Now my husband will live with me, because I have borne him six sons." She named him Zebulun(*Glorious dwelling*). ²¹Afterwards, she gave birth to a daughter, and named her Dinah(*Lover of justice*). ²²Our God remembered Rachel(*Lamb*), and our God listened to her, and opened her womb. ²³She conceived, gave birth to a son, and said, "Our God has taken away my reproach." ²⁴She named him Joseph(*May He add*), saying, "May Yahweh(*Jealous one*) add another son to me." ²⁵After Rachel(*Lamb*) had given birth to Joseph(*May He add*), Jacob(*Heel grabber*) said to Laban(*White*), "Send me away, that I may go to my own place, and to my country. ²⁶Give me my wives and my children for whom I have served you, and let me go; for you know my service with which I have served you." ²⁷Laban(*White*) said to him, "If now I have found favor in your eyes, stay here, for I have divined that Yahweh(*Jealous one*) has blessed me for your sake." ²⁸He said, "Appoint me your wages, and I will give it." ²⁹He said to him, "You know how I have served you, and how your livestock have fared with me. ³⁰For it was little which you had before I came, and it has increased to a multitude. Yahweh(*Jealous one*) has blessed you wherever I turned. Now when will I provide for my own house also?" ³¹He said, "What will I give you?" Jacob(*Heel grabber*) said, "You will not give me anything. If you will do this thing for me, I will again feed your flock and keep it. ³²I will pass through all your flock today, removing from there every speckled and spotted one, and every black one among the sheep, and the spotted and speckled among the goats. This will be my hire. ³³So my righteousness will answer for me hereafter, when you come concerning my hire that is before you. Every one that is not speckled and spotted among the goats, and black among the sheep, that might be with me, will be counted stolen." ³⁴Laban(*White*) said, "Behold, let it be according to your word." ³⁵That day, he removed the male goats that were streaked and spotted, and all the female goats that were speckled and spotted, every one that had white in it, and all the black ones among the sheep, and gave them into the hand of his sons. ³⁶He set three days' journey between himself and Jacob(*Heel grabber*), and Jacob(*Heel grabber*) fed the rest of the flock of Laban(

White). ³⁷Jacob(*Heel grabber*) took to himself rods of fresh poplar, almond, plane tree, peeled white streaks in them, and made the white appear which was in the rods. ³⁸He set the rods which he had peeled opposite the flocks in the gutters in the watering-troughs where the flocks came to drink. They conceived when they came to drink. ³⁹The flocks conceived before the rods, and the flocks produced streaked, speckled, and spotted. ⁴⁰Jacob(*Heel grabber*) separated the lambs, and set the faces of the flocks toward the streaked and all the black in the flock of Laban(*White*): and he put his own droves apart, and did not put them into the flock of Laban(*White*). ⁴¹Whenever the stronger of the flock conceived, Jacob(*Heel grabber*) laid the rods in front of the eyes of the flock in the gutters, that they might conceive among the rods; ⁴²but when the flock were feeble, he did not put them in. So the feebler belonged to Laban(*White*), and the stronger belonged to Jacob(*Heel grabber*). ⁴³The man increased exceedingly, and had large flocks, female servants and male servants, and camels and donkeys.

CHAPTER 31

¹He heard the words of the sons of Laban(*White*) saying, "Jacob(*Heel grabber*) has taken away all that was our father's. From that which was our father's, has he gotten all this wealth." ²Jacob(*Heel grabber*) saw the expression on the face of Laban(*White*) and, behold, it was not toward him as before. ³Yahweh(*Jealous one*) said to Jacob(*Heel grabber*), "Return to the land of your fathers, and to your relatives, and I will be with you." ⁴Jacob(*Heel grabber*) sent and called Rachel(*Lamb*) and Leah(*Wearied*) to the field to his flock, ⁵and said to them, "I see the expression on your father's face, that it is not toward me as before; but the God of my father has been with me. ⁶You know that I have served your father with all of my strength. ⁷Your father has deceived me, and changed my wages ten times, but our God did not allow him to hurt me. ⁸If he said this, 'The speckled will be your wages,' then all the flock gave birth to speckled. If he said this, 'The streaked will be your wages,' then all the flock gave birth to streaked. ⁹Thus our God has taken away your father's livestock, and given them to me. ¹⁰During mating season, I lifted up my eyes, and saw in a dream, and behold, the male goats which leaped on the flock were streaked, speckled, and grizzled. ¹¹The angel of our God said to me in the dream, 'Jacob(*Heel grabber*),' and I said, 'Here I am.' ¹²He said, 'Now lift up your eyes, and behold, all the male goats which leap on the flock are streaked, speckled, and grizzled, for I have seen all that Laban(*White*) does to you. ¹³I am the God of Bethel(*House of God*), where you anointed a pillar, where you vowed a vow to me. Now arise, get out from this land, and return to the land of your birth.'" ¹⁴Rachel(*Lamb*) and Leah(*Wearied*) answered him, "Is there yet any portion or inheritance for us in our father's house? ¹⁵Are not we accounted by him as foreigners? For he has sold us, and has also quite devoured our money. ¹⁶ For all the riches which our God has taken away from our father, that is ours and our children's. Now then, whatever our God has said to you, do." ¹⁷Then Jacob(*Heel grabber*) rose up, and set his sons and his wives on the camels, ¹⁸and he took away all his livestock, and all his pos-

sessions which he had gathered, including the livestock which he had gained in Paddan-Aram(*Elevated Plain*) to go to Isaac(*Laughter*) his father, to the land of Canaan(*Brought low*). ¹⁹ Now Laban(*White*) had gone to shear his sheep: and Rachel(*Lamb*) stole the Teraphim(*Nourishers*) that were her father's. ²⁰Jacob(*Heel grabber*) deceived Laban(*White*) the Syrian(*Elevated one*), in that he did not tell him that he was running away. ²¹So he fled with all that he had. He rose up, passed over the River, and set his face toward the mountain of Gilead(*Stone monument*). ²²Laban(*White*) was told on the third day that Jacob(*Heel grabber*) had fled. ²³He took his relatives with him, and pursued him seven days' journey. He overtook him in the mountain of Gilead(*Stone monument*). ²⁴Our God came to Laban(*White*), the Syrian(*Elevated one*), in a dream of the night, and said to him, "Be careful that you do not speak to Jacob(*Heel grabber*) either good or bad." ²⁵Laban(*White*) caught up with Jacob(*Heel grabber*). Now Jacob(*Heel grabber*) had pitched his tent in the mountain, and Laban(*White*) with his relatives encamped in the mountain of Gilead(*Stone monument*). ²⁶Laban(*White*) said to Jacob(*Heel grabber*), "What have you done, that you have deceived me, and carried away my daughters like captives of the sword? ²⁷Why did you flee secretly, and deceive me, and did not tell me, that I might have sent you away with mirth and with songs, with tambourine and with harp; ²⁸and did not allow me to kiss my sons and my daughters? Now have you done foolishly. ²⁹It is in the power of my hand to hurt you, but the God of your father spoke to me last night, saying, 'Be careful that you do not speak to Jacob(*Heel grabber*) either good or bad.' ³⁰Now, you want to be gone, because you greatly longed for your father's house, but why have you stolen my gods?" ³¹Jacob(*Heel grabber*) answered Laban(*White*), "Because I was afraid, for I said, 'Lest you should take your daughters from me by force.' ³²Anyone you find your gods with will not live. Before our relatives, discern what is yours with me, and take it." For Jacob(*Heel grabber*) did not know that Rachel(*Lamb*) had stolen them. ³³Laban(*White*) went into the tent of Jacob(*Heel grabber*), into the tent of Leah(*Wearied*), and into the tent of the two female servants; but he did not find them. He went out of tent of Leah(*Wearied*), and entered into the tent of Rachel(*Lamb*). ³⁴Now Rachel(*Lamb*) had taken the Teraphim(*Nourishers*), put them in the camel's saddle, and sat on them. Laban(*White*) felt around all the tent, but did not find them. ³⁵She said to her father, "Do not let my lord be angry that I cannot rise up before you; for I'm having my period." He searched, but did not find the Teraphim(*Nourishers*). ³⁶Jacob(*Heel grabber*) was angry, and argued with Laban(*White*). Jacob(*Heel grabber*) answered Laban(*White*), "What is my trespass? What is my sin, that you have hotly pursued me? ³⁷Now that you have felt around in all my stuff, what have you found of all your household stuff? Set it here before my relatives and your relatives, that they may judge between us two. ³⁸"These twenty years I have been with you. Your ewes and your female goats have not cast their young, and I have not eaten the rams of your flocks. ³⁹That which was torn of animals, I did not bring to you. I carried its loss. Of my hand you required it, whether stolen by day or stolen by night. ⁴⁰This was my situation: in the day the drought consumed me, and the frost by night; and my sleep fled from my eyes. ⁴¹These twenty years I have been in your house. I served you fourteen years for your two daughters, and six years for your flock, and you have changed my wages ten times. ⁴²Unless the God of my father, the God of Abraham(*Father of nations*), and the fear of Isaac(*Laughter*), had been with me, surely now you would have sent me away empty. Our God has seen my affliction and the labor of my hands, and rebuked you last night." ⁴³Laban(*White*) answered Jacob(*Heel grabber*), "The daughters are my daughters, the children are my children, the flocks are my flocks, and all that you see is mine: and what can I do today to these my daughters, or to their children whom they have borne? ⁴⁴Now come, let us make a covenant, you and I; and let it be for a witness between me and you." ⁴⁵Jacob(*Heel grabber*) took a stone, and set it up for a pillar. ⁴⁶Jacob(*Heel grabber*) said to his relatives, "Gather stones." They took stones, and made a heap. They ate there by the heap. ⁴⁷Laban(*White*) called it Jegar-Sahadutha(*Heap of witness*), but Jacob(*Heel grabber*) called it Galeed(*Heap of witness*). ⁴⁸Laban(*White*) said, "This heap is witness between me and you today." Therefore it was named Galeed(*Heap of witness*) ⁴⁹and Mizpah(*Watchtower*), for he said, "Yahweh(*Jealous one*)watch between me and you, when we are absent one from another. ⁵⁰If you afflict my daughters, or if you take wives besides my daughters, no man is with us; behold, our God is a witness between me and you." ⁵¹Laban(*White*) said to Jacob(*Heel grabber*), "See this heap, and see the pillar, which I have set between me and you. ⁵²May this heap be a witness, and the pillar be a witness, that I will not pass over this heap to you, and that you will not pass over this heap and this pillar to me, for harm. ⁵³The God of Abraham(*Father of na-*

tions), and the God of Nahor(*Snorting*), the God of their father, judge between us." Then Jacob(*Heel grabber*) swore by the fear of his father, Isaac(*Laughter*). ⁵⁴Jacob(*Heel grabber*) offered a sacrifice in the mountain, and called his relatives to eat bread. They ate bread, and stayed all night in the mountain. ⁵⁵Early in the morning, Laban(*White*) rose up, and kissed his sons and his daughters, and blessed them. Laban(*White*) departed and returned to his place.

CHAPTER 32

¹Jacob(*Heel grabber*) went on his way, and the angels of God met him. ²When he saw them, Jacob(*Heel grabber*) said, "This is the army of our God." He called the name of that place Mahanaim(*Two camps*). ³Jacob(*Heel grabber*) sent messengers in front of him to Esau(*Hairy*), his brother, to the land of Seir(*Goat*), the field of Edom(*Red*). ⁴He commanded them, saying, "This is what you will tell my lord, Esau(*Hairy*): 'This is what your servant, Jacob(*Heel grabber*), says. I have lived as a foreigner with Laban(*White*), and stayed until now. ⁵I have cattle, donkeys, flocks, male servants, and female servants. I have sent to tell my lord, that I may find favor in your sight.'" ⁶The messengers returned to Jacob(*Heel grabber*), saying, "We came to your brother Esau(*Hairy*). Not only that, but he comes to meet you, and four hundred men with him." ⁷Then Jacob(*Heel grabber*) was greatly afraid and was distressed. He divided the people who were with him, and the flocks, and the herds, and the camels, into two companies; ⁸and he said, "If Esau(*Hairy*) comes to the one company, and strikes it, then the company which is left will escape." ⁹Jacob(*Heel grabber*) said, "The God of my father Abraham(*Father of nations*), and the God of my father Isaac(*Laughter*), Yahweh(*Jealous one*), who said to me, 'Return to your country, and to your relatives, and I will do you good,' ¹⁰I am not worthy of the least of all the loving kindnesses, and of all the truth, which you have shown to your servant; for with just my staff I crossed over this Jordan(*Descending*); and now I have become two companies. ¹¹Please deliver me from the hand of my brother, from the hand of Esau(*Hairy*): for I fear him, unless he come and strike me, and the mothers with the children. ¹²You said, 'I will surely do you good, and make your offspring as the sand of the sea, which cannot be numbered because there are so many.'" ¹³He stayed there that night, and took from that which he had with him, a present for Esau(*Hairy*), his brother: ¹⁴two hundred female goats and twenty male goats, two hundred ewes and twenty rams, ¹⁵thirty milk camels and their colts, forty cows, ten bulls, twenty female donkeys and ten foals. ¹⁶He delivered them

into the hands of his servants, every herd by itself, and said to his servants, "Pass over before me, and put a space between herd and herd." ¹⁷He commanded the foremost, saying, "When Esau(*Hairy*), my brother, meets you, and asks you, saying, 'Whose are you? Where are you going? Whose are these before you?' ¹⁸Then you will say, 'They are of your servant, Jacob(*Heel grabber*). It is a present sent to my lord, Esau(*Hairy*). Behold, he also is behind us.'" ¹⁹He commanded also the second, and the third, and all that followed the herds, saying, "This is how you will speak to Esau(*Hairy*), when you find him. ²⁰You will say, 'Not only that, but behold, your servant, Jacob(*Heel grabber*), is behind us.'" For, he said, "I will appease him with the present that goes before me, and afterward I will see his face. Perhaps he will accept me." ²¹So the present passed over before him, and he himself stayed that night in the camp. ²²He rose up that night, and took his two wives, and his two servants, and his eleven sons, and crossed over the ford of the Jabbok(*Emptied*). ²³He took them, and sent them over the stream, and sent over that which he had. ²⁴Jacob(*Heel grabber*) was left alone, and wrestled with a man there until the breaking of the day. ²⁵When he saw that he did not prevail against him, he touched the hollow of his thigh, and the hollow of the thigh of Jacob(*Heel grabber*) was strained, as he wrestled. ²⁶The man said, "Let me go, for the day breaks." Jacob(*Heel grabber*) said, "I will not let you go, unless you bless me." ²⁷He said to him, "What is your name?" He said, "Jacob(*Heel grabber*)." ²⁸He said, "Your name will no longer be called Jacob(*Heel grabber*), but Israel(*Struggler with God*); for you have struggled with our God and men and have overcome." ²⁹Jacob(*Heel grabber*) asked him, "Please tell me your name." He said, "Why is it that you ask what my name is?" He blessed him there. ³⁰Jacob(*Heel grabber*) called the name of the place Peniel(*My God's face*): for, he said, "I have seen God face to face, and my life is preserved." ³¹The sun rose on him as he passed over Peniel(*My God's face*), and he limped because of his thigh. ³²Therefore the children of Israel(*Struggler with God*) do not eat the sinew of the hip, which is on the hollow of the thigh, to this day, because he touched the hollow of he thigh of Jacob(*Heel grabber*) in the sinew of the hip.

CHAPTER 33

¹Jacob(*Heel grabber*) lifted up his eyes, and looked, and, behold, Esau(*Hairy*) was coming, and with him four hundred men. He divided the children between Leah(*Wearied*), Rachel(*Lamb*), and the two servants. ²He put the servants and their children in front, Leah(*Wearied*) and her children after, and Rachel(*Lamb*) and Joseph(*May He add*) at the rear. ³He himself passed over in front of them, and bowed himself to the ground seven times, until he came near to his brother. ⁴Esau(*Hairy*) ran to meet him, embraced him, fell on his neck, kissed him, and they wept. ⁵He lifted up his eyes, and saw the women and the children; and said, "Who are these with you?" He said, "The children whom our God has graciously given your servant." ⁶Then the servants came near with their children, and they bowed themselves. ⁷Leah(*Wearied*) also and her children came near, and bowed themselves. After them, Joseph(*May He add*) came near with Rachel(*Lamb*), and they bowed themselves. ⁸Esau(*Hairy*) said, "What do you mean by all this company which I met?" Jacob(*Heel grabber*) said, "To find favor in the sight of my lord." ⁹Esau(*Hairy*) said, "I have enough, my brother; let that which you have be yours." ¹⁰Jacob(*Heel grabber*) said, "Please, no, if I have now found favor in your sight, then receive my present at my hand, because I have seen your face, as one sees the face of God, and you were pleased with me. ¹¹Please take the gift that I brought to you, because our God has dealt graciously with me, and because I have enough." He urged him, and he took it. ¹²Esau(*Hairy*) said, "Let us take our journey, and let us go, and I will go before you." ¹³Jacob(*Heel grabber*) said to him, "My lord knows that the children are tender, and that the flocks and herds with me have their young, and if they overdrive them one day, all the flocks will die. ¹⁴Please let my lord pass over before his servant, and I will lead on gently, according to the pace of the livestock that are before me and according to the pace of the children, until I come to my lord to Seir(*Goat*)." ¹⁵Esau(*Hairy*) said, "Let me now leave with you some of the folk who are with me." He said, "Why? Let me find favor in the sight of my lord." ¹⁶So

Esau(*Hairy*) returned that day on his way to Seir(*Goat*). ¹⁷Jacob(*Heel grabber*) traveled to Succoth(*Covered shelter*), built himself a house, and made shelters for his livestock. Therefore the name of the place is called Succoth(*Covered shelter*). ¹⁸Jacob(*Heel grabber*) came in peace to the city of Shechem(*Responsible*), which is in the land of Canaan(*Brought low*), when he came from Paddan-Aram(*Elevated plain*); and encamped before the city. ¹⁹He bought the parcel of ground where he had spread his tent, at the hand of the children of Hamor(*Donkey*), father of Shechem(*Responsible*), for one hundred pieces of money. ²⁰He erected an altar there, and called it El(*God*), Elohe(*God of*) Israel(*Struggler with God*).

CHAPTER 34

¹Dinah(*Lover of justice*), the daughter of Leah(*Wearied*), whom she bore Jacob(*Heel grabber*), went out to see the daughters of the land. ²Shechem(*Responsible*) the son of Hamor(*Donkey*) the Hivite(*Tent villager*), the prince of the land, saw her. He took her, lay with her, and humiliated her. ³His soul joined to Dinah(*Lover of justice*), the daughter of Jacob(*Heel grabber*), and he loved the young lady, and spoke kindly to the young lady. ⁴Shechem(*Responsible*) spoke to his father, Hamor(*Donkey*), saying, "Get me this young lady as a wife." ⁵ Now Jacob(*Heel grabber*) heard that he had defiled Dinah(*Lover of justice*), his daughter; and his sons were with his livestock in the field. Jacob(*Heel grabber*) held his peace until they came. ⁶Hamor(*Donkey*) the father of Shechem(*Responsible*) went out to Jacob(*Heel grabber*) to talk with him. ⁷The sons of Jacob(*Heel grabber*) came in from the field when they heard it. The men were grieved, and they were very angry, because he had done an outrageous thing in Israel(*Struggler with God*) by lying with the daughter of Jacob(*Heel grabber*); a thing ought not to be done. ⁸Hamor(*Donkey*) talked with them, saying, "The soul of my son, Shechem(*Responsible*) longs for your daughter. Please give her to him as a wife. ⁹Make marriages with us. Give your daughters to us, and take our daughters for yourselves. ¹⁰You will dwell with us, and the land will be before you. Live and trade in it, and get possessions in it." ¹¹Shechem(*Responsible*), said to her father and to her brothers, "Let me find favor in your eyes, and whatever you will tell me I will give. ¹²Ask me a great amount for a bride-price, and I will give whatever you ask of me, but give me the young lady as a wife." ¹³The sons of Jacob(*Heel grabber*) answered Shechem(*Responsible*) and Hamor(*Donkey*) his father with deceit, and spoke, because he had defiled Dinah(*Lover of justice*) their sister, ¹⁴and said to them, "We cannot do this thing, to give our sister to one who is uncircumcised; for that would be a disgrace to us. ¹⁵Only on this condition will we consent to you. If you will be as we are, that every male of you be circumcised; ¹⁶then will we give our daughters to you, and we will take your daughters

to us, and we will dwell with you, and we will become one people. ¹⁷But if you will not listen to us, to be circumcised, then we will take our sister, and we will be gone." ¹⁸Their words pleased Hamor(*Donkey*) and Shechem (*Responsible*) the son of Hamor(*Donkey*). ¹⁹The young man did not wait to do this thing, because he had delight in the daughter of Jacob(*Heel grabber*), and he was honored above all the house of his father. ²⁰Hamor(*Donkey*) and Shechem(*Responsible*), his son, came to the gate of their city, and talked with the men of their city, saying, ²¹"These men are peaceful with us. Therefore let them live in the land and trade in it. For behold, the land is large enough for them. Let us take their daughters to us for wives, and let us give them our daughters. ²²Only on this condition will the men consent to us to live with us, to become one people, if every male among us is circumcised, as they are circumcised. ²³Won't their livestock and their possessions and all their animals be ours? Only let us give our consent to them, and they will dwell with us." ²⁴All who went out of the gate of his city listened to Hamor(*Donkey*), and to Shechem(*Responsible*) his son; and every male was circumcised, all who went out of the gate of his city. ²⁵On the third day, when they were sore, two of the sons of Jacob(*Heel grabber*), Simeon(*One who heard and obeyed*) and Levi(*Attached*), brother of Dinah(*Lover of justice*), each took his sword, came upon the unsuspecting city, and killed all the males. ²⁶They killed Hamor(*Donkey*) and Shechem(*Responsible*), his son, with the edge of the sword, and took Dinah(*Lover of justice*) out of the house of Shechem(*Responsible*) and went away. ²⁷The sons of Jacob(*Heel grabber*) came on the dead, and plundered the city, because they had defiled their sister. ²⁸They took their flocks, their herds, their donkeys, that which was in the city, that which was in the field, ²⁹and all their wealth. They took captive all their little ones and their wives, and took as plunder everything that was in the house. ³⁰Jacob(*Heel grabber*) said to Simeon(*One who heard and obeyed*) and Levi(*Attached*), "You have troubled me, by making me a stink to the inhabitants of the land, among the Canaanites(*Ones brought low*) and the Perizzites(*Ones without boundaries*). I am few in number. They will gather themselves together against me and strike me, and I will be destroyed, I and my house." ³¹They said, "Should he deal with our sister as with a prostitute?"

CHAPTER 35

¹Our God said to Jacob(*Heel grabber*), "Arise, go up to Bethel(*House of God*), and live there. Make there an altar to God, who appeared to you when you fled from the face of Esau(*Hairy*) your brother." ²Then Jacob(*Heel grabber*) said to his household, and to all who were with him, "Put away the foreign gods that are among you, purify yourselves, change your garments. ³Let us arise, and go up to Bethel(*House of God*). I will make there an altar to God, who answered me in the day of my distress, and was with me on the way which I went." ⁴They gave to Jacob(*Heel grabber*) all the foreign gods which were in their hands, and the rings which were in their ears; and Jacob(*Heel grabber*) hid them under the oak which was by Shechem(*Responsible*). ⁵They traveled, and a terror of God was on the cities that were around them, and they did not pursue the sons of Jacob(*Heel grabber*). ⁶So Jacob(*Heel grabber*) came to Luz(*Almond tree*) [that is, Bethel (*House of God*)], which is in the land of Canaan(*Brought low*), he and all the people who were with him. ⁷He built an altar there, and called the place El-Bethel(*The God of the House of God*); because there our God was revealed to him, when he fled from the face of his brother. ⁸Deborah(*Word of Yahweh*), the nurse of Rebekah(*Securely bound*), died, and she was buried below Bethel(*House of God*) under the oak; and its name was called Allon-Bacuth(*Weeping oak tree*). ⁹Our God appeared to Jacob(*Heel grabber*) again, when he came from Paddan-Aram(*Elevated plain*) and blessed him. ¹⁰Our God said to him, "Your name is Jacob(*Heel grabber*). Your name will not be Jacob(*Heel grabber*) any more, but your name will be Israel(*Struggler with God*)." He named him Israel(*Struggler with God*). ¹¹Our God said to him, "I am the God who is enough. Be fruitful and multiply. A nation and a company of nations will be from you, and kings will come out of your body. ¹²The land which I gave to Abraham(*Father of nations*) and Isaac(*Laughter*), I will give it to you, and to your offspring after you will I give the land." ¹³Our God went up from him in the place where he spoke with him. ¹⁴Jacob(*Heel grabber*) set up a pillar in the place where he spoke with him, a

pillar of stone. He poured out a drink offering on it, and poured oil on it. **15**Jacob(*Heel grabber*) called the name of the place where God spoke with him "Bethel(*House of God*)." **16**They traveled from Bethel (*House of God*). There was still some distance to come to Ephrath(*Fruitful land*), and Rachel(*Lamb*) travailed. She had hard labor. **17**When she was in hard labor, the midwife said to her, "Do not be afraid, for now you will have another son." **18**As her soul was departing [for she died], she named him Benoni(*Son of calamity*), but his father named him Benjamin(*Son of my right hand*). **19**Rachel(*Lamb*) died, and was buried on the way to Ephrath(*Fruitful land*) [also called Bethlehem(*House of bread*)]. **20**Jacob(*Heel grabber*) set up a pillar on her grave. The same is the grave called "Pillar of Rachel(*Lamb*)" to this day. **21**Israel(*Struggler with God*) traveled, and spread his tent beyond the tower of Eder(*Flock*). **22**While Israel(*Struggler with God*) lived in that land, Reuben(*I see a son!*) went and lay with Bilhah(*Troubled*), his father's concubine, and Israel(*Struggler with God*) heard of it. Now the sons of Jacob(*Heel grabber*) were twelve. **23**The sons of Leah(*Wearied*): Reuben(*I see a son!*) [the firstborn of Jacob(*Heel grabber*)], Simeon(*One who heard and obeyed*), Levi(*Attached*), Judah(*One who praises*), Issachar(*Hired for wage*), and Zebulun(*Glorious dwelling*). **24**The sons of Rachel(*Lamb*): Joseph(*May He add*) and Benjamin(*Son of my right hand*). **25**The sons of Bilhah (*Troubled*) [servant of Rachel(*Lamb*)]: Dan(*One who judges*) and Naphtali(*My struggle*). **26**The sons of Zilpah(*A drop*) [servant of Leah(*Wearied*)]: Gad(*Fortunate*) and Asher(*Happy*). These are the sons of Jacob(*Heel grabber*), who were born to him in Paddan-Aram(*Elevated plain*). **27**Jacob(*Heel grabber*) came to Isaac(*Laughter*) his father, to Mamre(*Revealed from seeing*), to Kiriath-Arba(*Foursquared walled city*) [which is Hebron(*Alliance*)], where Abraham (*Father of nations*) and Isaac(*Laughter*) lived as foreigners. **28**The days of Isaac(*Laughter*) were one hundred eighty years. **29**Isaac(*Laughter*) gave up the spirit, and died, and was gathered to his people, old and full of days. Esau(*Hairy*) and Jacob(*Heel grabber*), his sons, buried him.

CHAPTER 36

¹Now this is the history of the generations of Esau(*Hairy*) [that is, Edom(*Red*)]. ²Esau(*Hairy*) took his wives from the daughters of Canaan(*Brought low*): Adah(*Adorned*) the daughter of Elon(*Mighty oak*), the Hittite(*Terrorist*); and Oholibamah(*My tent is a high place*) the daughter of Anah(*Answering*), the daughter of Zibeon(*One who uses dye*), the Hivite(*Tent villager*); ³and Basemath(*Perfumed*), daughter of Ishmael(*God listens*), sister of Nebaioth(*Prophecies*). ⁴Adah(*Adorned*) bore to Esau(*Hairy*) Eliphaz(*My God is pure gold*). Basemath(*Perfumed*) bore to Reuel(*Friend of God*). ⁵Oholibamah(*My tent is a high place*) bore to Jeush(*One who assembles*), Jalam(*He will hide*), and Korah(*Bald*). These are the sons of Esau(*Hairy*), who were born to him in the land of Canaan(*Brought low*). ⁶Esau(*Hairy*) took his wives, his sons, his daughters, and all the members of his household, with his livestock, all his animals, and all his possessions, which he had gathered in the land of Canaan(*Brought low*), and went into a land away from his brother Jacob(*Heel grabber*). ⁷For their substance was too great for them to dwell together, and the land of their travels could not bear them because of their livestock. ⁸Esau(*Hairy*) lived in the hill country of Seir(*Goat*). Esau(*Hairy*) is Edom(*Red*). ⁹This is the history of the generations of Esau(*Hairy*) the father of the Edomites(*Red ones*) in the hill country of Seir(*Goat*): ¹⁰these are the names of the sons of Esau(*Hairy*): Eliphaz(*My God is pure gold*), the son of Adah(*Adorned*), the wife of Esau(*Hairy*); and Reuel(*Friend of God*), the son of Basemath(*Perfumed*), the wife of Esau(*Hairy*). ¹¹The sons of Eliphaz (*My God is pure gold*) were Teman(*South*), Omar(*Talkative*), Zepho(*Watchful gaze*), and Gatam(*Fatigue*), and Kenaz(*Hunter*). ¹²Tikvah(*Withheld*) was concubine to Eliphaz(*My God is pure gold*), the son of Esau(*Hairy*); and she bore to Eliphaz(*My God is pure gold*) Amalek(*One who exhausts*). These are the sons of Adah(*Adorned*), wife of Esau(*Hairy*). ¹³These are the sons of Reuel(*Friend of God*): Nahath(*Rest*), Zerah(*Rising*), Shammah(*Born in a time of devastation*), and Mizzah(*Strength*). These were the sons of Basemath(*Perfumed*), wife of Es-

au(*Hairy*). **14**These were the sons of Oholibamah(*My tent is a high place*), the daughter of Anah(*Answering*), the daughter of Zibeon(*One who uses dye*), wife of Esau(*Hairy*): she bore to Esau(*Hairy*) Jeush(*One who assembles*), Jalam(*He will hide*), and Korah(*Bald*). **15**These are the chiefs of the sons of Esau(*Hairy*): the sons of Eliphaz(*My God is pure gold*) the firstborn of Esau(*Hairy*): chief Teman(*South*), chief Omar(*Talkative*), chief Zepho(*Watchful gaze*), chief Kenaz(*Hunter*), **16**chief Korah(*Bald*), chief Gatam(*Fatigue*), chief Amalek(*One who exhausts*): these are the chiefs who came of Eliphaz(*My God is pure gold*) in the land of Edom(*Red*); these are the sons of Adah(*Adorned*). **17**These are the sons of Reuel(*Friend of God*), son fo Esau(*Hairy*): chief Nahath(*Rest*), chief Zerah(*Rising*), chief Shammah(*Born in a time of devastation*), chief Mizzah(*Strength*): these are the chiefs who came of Reuel(*Friend of God*) in the land of Edom(*Red*); these are the sons of Basemath(*Perfumed*), wife of Esau(*Hairy*). **18**These are the sons of Oholibamah(*My tent is a high place*), wife of Esau(*Hairy*): chief Jeush(*One who assembles*), chief Jalam(*He will hide*), chief Korah(*Bald*): these are the chiefs who came of Oholibamah(*My tent is a high place*) the daughter of Anah(*Answering*), wife of Esau(*Hairy*). **19**These are the sons of Esau(*Hairy*) [that is, Edom(*Red*)], and these are their chiefs. **20**These are the sons of Seir(*Goat*) the Horite(*Cave user*), the inhabitants of the land: Lotan(*One covered*), Shobal(*Flowing*), Zibeon(*One who uses dye*), Anah(*Answering*), **21**Dishon(*Antelope*), Ezer(*Help*), and Dishan(*Antelope*). These are the chiefs who came of the Horites(*Cave users*), the children of Seir(*Goat*) in the land of Edom(*Red*). **22**The children of Lotan(*One covered*) were Hori(*My cave*) and Hemam(*Destruction*). The sister of Lotan(*One covered*) was Tikvah(*Withheld*). **23**These are the children of Shobal(*Flowing*): Alvan(*Unrighteous*), Manahath(*Place of rest*), Ebal(*Stone*), Shepho(*Barren place*), and Onam(*Their weariness*). **24**These are the children of Zibeon(*One who uses dye*): Aiah(*Little hawk*) and Anah(*Answering*). This is Anah(*Answering*) who found the hot springs in the wilderness, as he fed the donkeys of Zibeon(*One who uses dye*) his father. **25**These are the children of Anah(*Answering*): Dishon(*Antelope*) and Oholibamah(*My tent is a high place*), the daughter of Anah (*Answering*). **26**These are the children of Dishon(*Antelope*): Hemdan(*Delighted*), Eshban (*Man of understanding*), Ithran(*Surplus*), and Cheran(*Union*). **27**These are the children of Ezer(*Help*): Bilhan(*Tender*), Zaavan(*Highly agitated*), and Akan(*Twisted*). **28**These are the children of Dishan(Antelope): Uz(*Counsel*) and Aran(*Wild goat*). **29**These are the chiefs who came of the Horites(*Cave users*): chief Lotan(*One covered*), chief Shobal(*Flowing*), chief Zibeon(*One who uses dye*), chief Anah(*Answering*), ³⁰chief Dishon(*Antelope*), chief Ezer(*Help*), and chief Dishan(*Antelope*): these are the chiefs who came of the Horites(*Cave users*), according to their chiefs in the land of Seir(*Goat*). ³¹These are the kings who reigned in the land of Edom(*Red*), before any king reigned over the children of Israel(*Struggler with God*). ³²Bela(*Devouring*), the son of Beor(*Torch*), reigned in Edom(*Red*). The name of his city was Dinhabah(*Gives judgement*). ³³Bela(*Devouring*) died, and Jobab(*One who howls*), the son of Zerah(*Rising*) of Bozrah(*Sheep pen*), reigned in his place. ³⁴Jobab(*One who howls*), died, and Husham(*Great urgency*) of the land of the Temanites(*Southerners*) reigned in his place. ³⁵Husham(*Great urgency*) died, and Hadad(*Sharpened*), the son of Bedad(*Separate*), who struck Midian(*Strife*) in the field of Moab(*Unknown father*), reigned in his place. The name of his city was Avith(*Ruins*). ³⁶Hadad(*Sharpened*) died, and Samlah(*Robe*) of Masrekah(*Vineyard*) reigned in his place. ³⁷Samlah(*Robe*) died, and Shaul(*Asked for*) of Rehoboth(*Spacious*) by the river, reigned in his place. ³⁸ Shaul(*Asked for*) died, and Baal-Hanan(*Gracious lord*), the son of Achbor(*Mouse*) reigned in his place. ³⁹Baal-Hanan(*Gracious lord*) the son of Achbor (*Mouse*) died, and Hadar(*Ornament*) reigned in his place. The name of his city was Pau(*Crying out*). His wife's name was Mehatabel(*Good for God*), the daughter of Matred(*Constant pursuit*), the daughter of Mezahab(*Waters of gold*). ⁴⁰These are the names of the chiefs who came from Esau(*Hairy*), according to their families, after their places, and by their names: chief Tikvah(*Withheld*), chief Alvah(*Rising*), chief Jetheth(*One who shouts*), ⁴¹chief Oholibamah(*My tent is a high place*), chief Elah(*Mighty oak tree*), chief Pinon(*Pearls*), ⁴²chief Kenaz(*Hunter*), chief Teman(*South*), chief Mibzar(*Fortified*), ⁴³chief Magdiel(*Best gift of God*), and chief Iram(*City of people*). These are the chiefs of Edom(*Red*), according to their habitations in the land of their possession. This is Esau(*Hairy*), the father of the Edomites(*Red Ones*).

CHAPTER 37

¹Jacob(*Heel grabber*) lived in the land of his father's travels, in the land of Canaan(*Brought low*). ²This is the history of the generations of Jacob(*Heel grabber*). Joseph(*May He add*), being seventeen years old, was feeding the flock with his brothers. He was a boy with the sons of Bilhah(*Troubled*) and Zilpah(*A drop*), his father's wives. Joseph(*May He add*) brought an evil report of them to their father. ³Now Israel(*Struggler with God*) loved Joseph(*May He add*) more than all his children, because he was the son of his old age, and he made him a coat of many colors. ⁴His brothers saw that their father loved him more than all his brothers, and they hated him, and could not speak peaceably to him. ⁵Joseph(*May He add*) dreamed a dream, and he told it to his brothers, and they hated him all the more. ⁶He said to them, "Please hear this dream which I have dreamed: ⁷for behold, we were binding sheaves in the field, and behold, my sheaf arose and also stood upright; and behold, your sheaves came around, and bowed down to my sheaf." ⁸His brothers said to him, "Will you indeed reign over us? Or will you indeed have dominion over us?" They hated him all the more for his dreams and for his words. ⁹He dreamed yet another dream, and told it to his brothers, and said, "Behold, I have dreamed yet another dream: and behold, the sun and the moon and eleven stars bowed down to me." ¹⁰He told it to his father and to his brothers. His father rebuked him, and said to him, "What is this dream that you have dreamed? Will I and your mother and your brothers indeed come to bow ourselves down to you to the earth?" ¹¹His brothers envied him, but his father kept this saying in mind. ¹²His brothers went to feed their father's flock in Shechem(*Responsible*). ¹³Israel(*Struggler with God*) said to Joseph(*May He add*), "Are not your brothers feeding the flock in Shechem(*Responsible*)? Come, and I will send you to them." He said to him, "Here I am." ¹⁴He said to him, "Go now, see whether it is well with your brothers, and well with the flock; and bring me word again." So he sent him out of the valley of Hebron(*Alliance*), and he came to Shechem(*Responsible*). ¹⁵A certain man found him, and

behold, he was wandering in the field. The man asked him, "What are you looking for?" ⁱ⁶He said, "I am looking for my brothers. Tell me, please, where they are feeding the flock." ¹⁷The man said, "They have left here, for I heard them say, 'Let us go to Dothan(*Two wells*).'" Joseph(*May He add*) went after his brothers, and found them in Dothan(*Two wells*). ¹⁸They saw him afar off, and before he came near to them, they conspired against him to kill him. ¹⁹They said to one another, "Behold, this dreamer comes. ²⁰Come now therefore, and let's kill him, and cast him into one of the pits, and we will say, 'An evil beast has devoured him.' We will see what will become of his dreams." ²¹Reuben(*I see a son!*) heard it, and delivered him out of their hand, and said, "Let's not take his life." ²²Reuben(*I see a son!*) said to them, "Shed no blood. Throw him into this pit that is in the wilderness, but lay no hand on him"—that he might deliver him out of their hand, to restore him to his father. ²³When Joseph(*May He add*) came to his brothers, they stripped Joseph(*May He add*) of his coat, the coat of many colors that was on him; ²⁴and they took him, and threw him into the pit. The pit was empty. There was no water in it. ²⁵They sat down to eat bread, and they lifted up their eyes and looked, and saw a caravan of Ishmaelites(*Ones whom God listens*) was coming from Gilead(*Stone monument*), with their camels bearing spices and balm and myrrh, going to carry it down to Egypt(*Double anxiety*). ²⁶Judah(*One who praises*) said to his brothers, "What profit is it if we kill our brother and conceal his blood? ²⁷Come, and let's sell him to the Ishmaelites(*Ones whom God listens*), and not let our hand be on him; for he is our brother, our flesh." His brothers listened to him. ²⁸Midianites(*Ones in strife*) who were merchants passed by, and they drew and lifted up Joseph(*May He add*) out of the pit, and sold Joseph(*May He add*) to the Ishmaelites(*Ones whom God listens*) for twenty pieces of silver. They brought Joseph(*May He add*) into Egypt(*Double anxiety*). ²⁹Reuben(*I see a son!*) returned to the pit; and saw that Joseph(*May He add*) was not in the pit; and he tore his clothes. ³⁰He returned to his brothers, and said, "The child is no more; and I, where will I go?" ³¹They took the coat of Joseph(*May He add*) coat, and killed a male goat, and dipped the coat in the blood. ³²They took the coat of many colors, and they brought it to their father, and said, "We have found this. Examine it, now, whether it is your son's coat or not." ³³He recognized it, and said, "It is my son's coat. An evil beast has devoured him. Joseph(*May He add*) is without doubt torn in pieces." ³⁴Jacob(*Heel grabber*) tore his clothes, and put sackcloth on his waist, and mourned for his son many days. ³⁵All his sons and all his daughters rose up to comfort him, but he refused to be comforted. He said, "For I will go down to Sheol(*Asked for*) to my son mourning." His father wept for him. ³⁶The Midianites(*Ones in strife*) sold him into Egypt(*Double anxiety*) to Potiphar(*Given by the sun god),* an officer of Pharaoh's, the captain of the guard.

CHAPTER 38

¹At that time, Judah(*One who praises*) went down from his brothers, and visited a certain Adullamite(*Justice of the people*), whose name was Hirah(*Noble*). ²Judah(*One who praises*) saw there a daughter of a certain Canaanite(*One brought low*) whose name was Shua(*Crying out*). He took her, and went in to her. ³She conceived, and gave birth to a son; and he named him Er(*Awakened to watch*). ⁴She conceived again, and gave birth to a son; and she named him Onan(*Their trouble*). ⁵She yet again gave birth to a son, and named him Shelah(*Prayer*): and he was at Chezib(*Deceit*), when she gave birth to him. ⁶Judah(*Praise*) took a wife for Er(*Awakened to watch*), his firstborn, and her name was Tamar(*Palm tree*). ⁷Er (*Awaken to watch*), the firstborn of Judah(*One who praises*), was wicked in the sight of Yahweh(*Jealous one*). Yahweh(*Jealous one*) killed him. ⁸Judah(*One who praises*) said to Onan(*Their trouble*), "Go in to your brother's wife, and perform the duty of a husband's brother to her, and raise up offspring for your brother." ⁹Onan(*Their trouble*) knew that the offspring would not be his; and when he went in to his brother's wife, he spilled it on the ground, unless he should give offspring to his brother. ¹⁰The thing which he did was evil in the sight of Yahweh(*Jealous one*) and he killed him also. ¹¹Then Judah(*One who praises*) said to Tamar(*Palm tree*), his daughter-in-law, "Remain a widow in your father's house, until Shelah(*Prayer*), my son, is grown up"; for he said, "Lest he also die, like his brothers." Tamar(*Palm tree*) went and lived in her father's house. ¹²After many days, the daughter of Shua(*Crying out*), the wife of Judah(*One who praises*), died. Judah(*One who praises*) was comforted, and went up to his sheep shearers to Tikvah(*Withheld*), he and his friend Hirah(*Noble*), the Adullamite(*Justice of the people*). ¹³Tamar(*Palm tree*) was told, "Behold, your father-in-law is going up to Tikvah(*Withheld*) to shear his sheep." ¹⁴She took off of her the garments of her widowhood, and covered herself with her veil, and wrapped herself, and sat in the gate of Enaim(*Two fountains*), which is by the way to Tikvah(*Withheld*); for she saw that Shelah(*Prayer*) was grown up, and she

was not given to him as a wife. ¹⁵When Judah(*One who praises*) saw her, he thought that she was a prostitute, for she had covered her face. ¹⁶He turned to her by the way, and said, "Please come, let me come in to you," for he did not know that she was his daughter-in-law. She said, "What will you give me, that you may come in to me?" ¹⁷He said, "I will send you a young goat from the flock." She said, "Will you give me a pledge, until you send it?" ¹⁸He said, "What pledge will I give you?" She said, "Your signet and your cord, and your staff that is in your hand." He gave them to her, and came in to her, and she conceived by him. ¹⁹She arose, and went away, and put off her veil from her, and put on the garments of her widowhood. ²⁰Judah(*One who praises*) sent the young goat by the hand of his friend, the Adullamite(*Justice of the people*), to receive the pledge from the woman's hand, but he did not find her. ²¹Then he asked the men of her place, saying, "Where is the prostitute, that was at Enaim(*Two fountains*) by the road?" They said, "There has been no prostitute here." ²²He returned to Judah(*One who praises*), and said, "I have not found her; and also the men of the place said, 'There has been no prostitute here.'" ²³ Judah(*One who praises*) said, "Let her keep it, unless we be shamed. Behold, I sent this young goat, and you have not found her." ²⁴About three months later, Judah(*One who praises*) was told, "Tamar(*Palm tree*), your daughter-in-law, has played the prostitute. Moreover, behold, she is with child by prostitution." Judah(*One who praises*) said, "Bring her out, and let her be burned." ²⁵When she was brought out, she sent to her father-in-law, saying, "By the man, whose these are, I am with child." She also said, "Please discern whose are these—the signet, and the cords, and the staff." ²⁶ Judah(*One who praises*) acknowledged them, and said, "She is more righteous than I, because I did not give her to Shelah(*Prayer*), my son." He knew her again no more. ²⁷In the time of her travail, behold, twins were in her womb. ²⁸When she travailed, one put out a hand, and the midwife took and tied a scarlet thread on his hand, saying, "This came out first." ²⁹As he drew back his hand, behold, his brother came out, and she said, "Why have you made a breach for yourself?" Therefore his name was called Perez(*Breakthrough*). ³⁰Afterward his brother came out, that had the scarlet thread on his hand, and his name was called Zerah(*Rising*).

CHAPTER 39

¹Joseph(*May He add*) was brought down to Egypt(*Double anxiety*). Potiphar(*Given by the sun god*), an officer of Pharaoh's, the captain of the guard, an Egyptian(*Much anxious one*), bought him from the hand of the Ishmaelites(*Ones whom God listens*) that had brought him down there. ²Yahweh(*Jealous one*) was with Joseph(*May He add*), and he was a prosperous man. He was in the house of his master the Egyptian(*Much anxious one*). ³His master saw that Yahweh(*Jealous one*) was with him, and that Yahweh(*Jealous one*) made all that he did prosper in his hand. ⁴Joseph(*May He add*) found favor in his sight. He ministered to him, and he made him overseer over his house, and all that he had he put into his hand. ⁵From the time that he made him overseer in his house, and over all that he had, Yahweh(*Jealous one*) blessed the house of the Egyptian(*Much anxious one*) for the sake of Joseph(*May He add*). The blessing of Yahweh*Jealous one*) was on all that he had, in the house and in the field. ⁶He left all that he had in the hand of Joseph(*May He add*). He did not concern himself with anything, except for the food which he ate. Joseph(*May He add*) was well-built and handsome. ⁷After these things, his master's wife set her eyes on Joseph(*May He add*); and she said, "Lie with me." ⁸But he refused, and said to his master's wife, "Behold, my master doesn't know what is with me in the house, and he has put all that he has into my hand. ⁹No one is greater in this house than I am, and he has not kept back anything from me but you, because you are his wife. How then can I do this great wickedness, and sin against our God?" ¹⁰As she spoke to Joseph(*May He add*) day by day, he did not listen to her, to lie by her, or to be with her. ¹¹About this time, he went into the house to do his work, and there were none of the men of the house inside. ¹²She caught him by his garment, saying, "Lie with me!" He left his garment in her hand, and ran outside. ¹³When she saw that he had left his garment in her hand, and had run outside, ¹⁴she called to the men of her house, and spoke to them, saying, "Behold, he has brought in a Hebrew(*One passing over*) to us to harass us. He came in to me to lie with me, and I

cried with a loud voice. ¹⁵When he heard that I lifted up my voice and cried, he left his garment by me, and ran outside." ¹⁶She laid up his garment by her, until his master came home. ¹⁷She spoke to him according to these words, saying, "The Hebrew(*One passing over*) servant, whom you have brought to us, came into me to harass me, ¹⁸and as I lifted up my voice and cried, he left his garment by me, and ran outside." ¹⁹When his master heard the words of his wife, which she spoke to him, saying, "This is what your servant did to me," his wrath was kindled. ²⁰The master of Joseph(*May He add*) took him, and put him into the prison, the place where the king's prisoners were bound, and he was there in custody. ²¹But Yahweh(*Jealous one*) was with Joseph(*May He add*), and showed kindness to him, and gave him favor in the sight of the keeper of the prison. ²²The keeper of the prison committed to the hand of Joseph(*May He add*) all the prisoners who were in the prison. Whatever they did there, he was responsible for it. ²³The keeper of the prison did not look after anything that was under his hand, because Yahweh(*Jealous one*) was with him; and that which he did, Yahweh(*Jealous one*) made it prosper.

CHAPTER 40

¹After these things, the butler of the king of Egypt(*Double anxiety*) and his baker offended their lord, the king of Egypt(*Double anxiety*). ²Pharaoh was angry with his two officers, the chief cup bearer and the chief baker. ³He put them in custody in the house of the captain of the guard, into the prison, the place where Joseph(*May He add*) was bound. ⁴The captain of the guard assigned them to Joseph(*May He add*), and he took care of them. They stayed in prison many days. ⁵They both dreamed a dream, each man his dream, in one night, each man according to the interpretation of his dream, the cup bearer and the baker of the king of Egypt(*Double anxiety*), who were bound in the prison. ⁶Joseph(*May He add*) came in to them in the morning, and saw them, and saw that they were sad. ⁷He asked Pharaoh's officers who were with him in custody in his master's house, saying, "Why do you look so sad today?" ⁸They said to him, "We have dreamed a dream, and there is no one who can interpret it." Joseph(*May He add*) said to them, "Do not interpretations belong to our God? Please tell it to me." ⁹The chief cup bearer told his dream to Joseph(*May He add*), and said to him, "In my dream, behold, a vine was in front of me, ¹⁰and in the vine were three branches. It was as though it budded, it blossomed, and its clusters produced ripe grapes. ¹¹Pharaoh's cup was in my hand; and I took the grapes, and pressed them into Pharaoh's cup, and I gave the cup into Pharaoh's hand." ¹²Joseph(*May He add*) said to him, "This is its interpretation: the three branches are three days. ¹³Within three more days, Pharaoh will lift up your head, and restore you to your office. You will give Pharaoh's cup into his hand, the way you did when you were his cup bearer. ¹⁴But remember me when it will be well with you, and please show kindness to me, and make mention of me to Pharaoh, and bring me out of this house. ¹⁵For indeed, I was stolen away out of the land of the Hebrews(*Ones passing over*), and here also have I done nothing that they should put me into the dungeon." ¹⁶When the chief baker saw that the interpretation was good, he said to Joseph(*May He add*), "I also was in my dream, and behold,

three baskets of white bread were on my head. ¹⁷In the uppermost basket there were all kinds of baked food for Pharaoh, and the birds ate them out of the basket on my head." ¹⁸Joseph(*May He add*) answered, "This is its interpretation. The three baskets are three days. ¹⁹Within three more days, Pharaoh will lift up your head from off you, and will hang you on a tree; and the birds will eat your flesh from off you." ²⁰On the third day, which was Pharaoh's birthday, he made a feast for all his servants, and he lifted up the head of the chief cup bearer and the head of the chief baker among his servants. ²¹He restored the chief cup bearer to his position again, and he gave the cup into Pharaoh's hand; ²²but he hanged the chief baker, as Joseph(*May He add*) had interpreted to them. ²³Yet the chief cup bearer did not remember Joseph(*May He add*), but forgot him.

CHAPTER 41

¹At the end of two full years, Pharaoh dreamed: and behold, he stood by the river. ²Behold, there came up out of the river seven cattle, sleek and fat, and they fed in the marsh grass. ³Behold, seven other cattle came up after them out of the river, ugly and thin, and stood by the other cattle on the brink of the river. ⁴The ugly and thin cattle ate up the seven sleek and fat cattle. So Pharaoh awoke. ⁵He slept and dreamed a second time: and behold, seven heads of grain came up on one stalk, healthy and good. ⁶Behold, seven heads of grain, thin and blasted with the east wind, sprung up after them. ⁷The thin heads of grain swallowed up the seven healthy and full ears. Pharaoh awoke, and behold, it was a dream. ⁸In the morning, his spirit was troubled, and he sent and called for all of the magicians of Egypt(*Double anxiety*) magicians and wise men. Pharaoh told them his dreams, but there was no one who could interpret them to Pharaoh. ⁹Then the chief cup bearer spoke to Pharaoh, saying, "I remember my faults today. ¹⁰Pharaoh was angry with his servants, and put me in custody in the house of the captain of the guard, me and the chief baker. ¹¹We dreamed a dream in one night, I and he. We dreamed each man according to the interpretation of his dream. ¹²There was with us there a young man, a Hebrew(*One passing over*), servant to the captain of the guard, and we told him, and he interpreted to us our dreams. To each man according to his dream he interpreted. ¹³As he interpreted to us, so it was. He restored me to my office, and he hanged him." ¹⁴Then Pharaoh sent and called Joseph(*May He add*), and they brought him hastily out of the dungeon. He shaved himself, changed his clothing, and came in to Pharaoh. ¹⁵Pharaoh said to Joseph(*May He add*), "I have dreamed a dream, and there is no one who can interpret it. I have heard it said of you, that when you hear a dream you can interpret it." ¹⁶Joseph(*May He add*) answered Pharaoh, saying, "It is not in me. Our God will give Pharaoh an answer of peace." ¹⁷Pharaoh spoke to Joseph(*May He add*), "In my dream, behold, I stood on the brink of the river: ¹⁸and behold, there came up out of the river seven cattle, fat and sleek.

They fed in the marsh grass, ¹⁹and behold, seven other cattle came up after them, poor and very ugly and thin, such as I never saw in all the land of Egypt(*Double anxiety*) for ugliness. ²⁰The thin and ugly cattle ate up the first seven fat cattle, ²¹and when they had eaten them up, it could not be known that they had eaten them, but they were still ugly, as at the beginning. So I awoke. ²²I saw in my dream, and behold, seven heads of grain came up on one stalk, full and good: ²³and behold, seven heads of grain, withered, thin, and blasted with the east wind, sprung up after them. ²⁴The thin heads of grain swallowed up the seven good heads of grain. I told it to the magicians, but there was no one who could explain it to me." ²⁵Joseph(*May He add*) said to Pharaoh, "The dream of Pharaoh is one. What our God is about to do he has declared to Pharaoh. ²⁶The seven good cattle are seven years; and the seven good heads of grain are seven years. The dream is one. ²⁷The seven thin and ugly cattle that came up after them are seven years, and also the seven empty heads of grain blasted with the east wind; they will be seven years of famine. ²⁸That is the thing which I spoke to Pharaoh. What our God is about to do he has shown to Pharaoh. ²⁹Behold, there come seven years of great plenty throughout all the land of Egypt(*Double anxiety*). ³⁰There will arise after them seven years of famine, and all the plenty will be forgotten in the land of Egypt(*Double anxiety*). The famine will consume the land, ³¹and the plenty will not be known in the land by reason of that famine which follows; for it will be very grievous. ³²The dream was doubled to Pharaoh, because the thing is established by our God, and our God will shortly bring it to pass. ³³"Now therefore let Pharaoh look for a discreet and wise man, and set him over the land of Egypt(*Double anxiety*). ³⁴Let Pharaoh do this, and let him appoint overseers over the land, and take up the fifth part of the land of the produce of Egypt(*Double anxiety*) in the seven plenteous years. ³⁵Let them gather all the food of these good years that come, and lay up grain under the hand of Pharaoh for food in the cities, and let them keep it. ³⁶The food will be for a store to the land against the seven years of famine, which will be in the land of Egypt(*Double anxiety*); that the land not perish through the famine." ³⁷The thing was good in the eyes of Pharaoh, and in the eyes of all his servants. ³⁸Pharaoh said to his servants, "Can we find such a one as this, a man in whom is the Spirit of our God?" ³⁹Pharaoh said to Joseph(*May He add*), "Because our God has shown you all of this, there is no one so discreet and wise as you. ⁴⁰

You will be over my house, and according to your word will all my people be ruled. Only in the throne I will be greater than you." ⁴¹Pharaoh said to Joseph(*May He add*), "Behold, I have set you over all the land of Egypt(*Double anxiety*)." ⁴²Pharaoh took off his signet ring from his hand, and put it on the hand of Joseph(*May He add*), and arrayed him in robes of fine linen, and put a gold chain about his neck, ⁴³and he made him to ride in the second chariot which he had. They proclaimed before him, "Bow the knee!" He set him over all the land of Egypt(*Double anxiety*). ⁴⁴Pharaoh said to Joseph(*May He add*), "I am Pharaoh, and without you will no man lift up his hand or his foot in all the land of Egypt(*Double anxiety*)." ⁴⁵Pharaoh called the name of Joseph(*May He add*) Zaphenath-Paneah(*Concealed treasure*); and he gave him Asenath(*Mischief*), the daughter of Potiphera(*Whom the sun god gave*) priest of On(*Pillar*) as a wife. Joseph(*May He add*) went out over the land of Egypt(*Double anxiety*). ⁴⁶Joseph(*May He add*) was thirty years old when he stood before Pharaoh king of Egypt(*Double anxiety*). Joseph(*May He add*) went out from the presence of Pharaoh, and went throughout all the land of Egypt(*Double anxiety*). ⁴⁷In the seven plenteous years the earth produced abundantly. ⁴⁸He gathered up all the food of the seven years which were in the land of Egypt(*Double anxiety*), and laid up the food in the cities: the food of the field, which was around every city, he laid up in the same. ⁴⁹Joseph(*May He add*) laid up grain as the sand of the sea, very much, until he stopped counting, for it was without number. ⁵⁰To Joseph(*May He add*) were born two sons before the year of famine came, whom Asenath(*Mischief*), the daughter of Potiphera(*Whom the sun god gave*) priest of On(*Pillar*), bore to him. ⁵¹Joseph(*May He add*) called the name of the firstborn Manasseh(*Made to forget*), "For", he said, "Our God has made me forget all my toil, and all my father's house." ⁵²The name of the second, he called Ephraim(*Very fruitful*): "For our God has made me fruitful in the land of my affliction." ⁵³The seven years of plenty, that were in the land of Egypt(*Double anxiety*), came to an end. ⁵⁴The seven years of famine began to come, just as Joseph(*May He add*) had said. There was famine in all lands, but in all the land of Egypt(*Double anxiety*) there was bread. ⁵⁵When all the land of Egypt(*Double anxiety*) was famished, the people cried to Pharaoh for bread, and Pharaoh said to all the Egyptians(*Much anxious ones*), "Go to Joseph(*May He add*). What he says to you, do." ⁵⁶The famine was over all the surface of the earth. Joseph(*May He add*) opened all the store houses, and sold to the Egyptians(*Much *anxious ones*). The famine was severe in the land of Egypt(*Double anxiety*). ⁵⁷All countries came into Egypt(*Double anxiety*), to Joseph(*May He add*), to buy grain, because the famine was severe in all the earth.

CHAPTER 42

¹Now Jacob(*Heel grabber*) saw that there was grain in Egypt(*Double anxiety*), and Jacob(*Heel grabber*) said to his sons, "Why do you look at one another?" ²He said, "Behold, I have heard that there is grain in Egypt(*Double anxiety*). Go down there, and buy for us from there, so that we may live, and not die." ³The ten brothers of Joseph(*May He add*) went down to buy grain from Egypt(*Double anxiety*). ⁴But Jacob(*Heel grabber*) did not send Benjamin(*Son of my right hand*), the brother of Joseph(*May He add*), with his brothers; for he said, "Lest perhaps harm happen to him." ⁵The sons of Israel(*Struggler with God*) came to buy among those who came, for the famine was in the land of Canaan(*Brought low*). ⁶Joseph(*May He add*) was the governor over the land. It was he who sold to all the people of the land. The brothers of Joseph(*May He add*) came, and bowed themselves down to him with their faces to the earth. ⁷Joseph(*May He add*) saw his brothers, and he recognized them, but acted like a stranger to them, and spoke roughly with them. He said to them, "Where did you come from?" They said, "From the land of Canaan(*Brought low*) to buy food." ⁸Joseph(*May He add*) recognized his brothers, but they did not recognize him. ⁹Joseph(*May He add*) remembered the dreams which he dreamed about them, and said to them, "You are spies! You have come to see the nakedness of the land." ¹⁰They said to him, "No, my lord, but your servants have come to buy food. ¹¹We are all one man's sons; we are honest men. Your servants are not spies." ¹²He said to them, "No, but you have come to see the nakedness of the land!" ¹³They said, "We, your servants, are twelve brothers, the sons of one man in the land of Canaan(*Brought low*); and behold, the youngest is today with our father, and one is no more." ¹⁴Joseph(*May He add*) said to them, "It is like I told you, saying, 'You are spies!' ¹⁵By this you will be tested. By the life of Pharaoh, you will not go out from here, unless your youngest brother comes here. ¹⁶Send one of you, and let him get your brother, and you will be bound, that your words may be tested, whether there is truth in you, or else by the life of Pharaoh surely you are spies." ¹⁷He put them all to-

gether into custody for three days. ¹⁸Joseph(*May He add*) said to them the third day, "Do this, and live, for I fear our God. ¹⁹If you are honest men, then let one of your brothers be bound in your prison; but you go, carry grain for the famine of your houses. ²⁰Bring your youngest brother to me; so will your words be verified, and you will not die." They did so. ²¹They said to one another, "We are certainly guilty concerning our brother, in that we saw the distress of his soul, when he begged us, and we would not listen. Therefore this distress has come upon us." ²²Reuben(*I see a son!*) answered them, saying, "Did not I tell you, saying, 'Do not sin against the child,' and you would not listen? Therefore also, behold, his blood is required." ²³They did not know that Joseph(*May He add*) understood them; for there was an interpreter between them. ²⁴He turned himself away from them, and wept. Then he returned to them, and spoke to them, and took Simeon(*One who heard and obeyed*) from among them, and bound him before their eyes. ²⁵Then Joseph(*May He add*) gave a command to fill their bags with grain, and to restore each man's money into his sack, and to give them food for the way. So it was done to them. ²⁶They loaded their donkeys with their grain, and departed from there. ²⁷As one of them opened his sack to give his donkey food in the lodging place, he saw his money. Behold, it was in the mouth of his sack. ²⁸He said to his brothers, "My money is restored! Behold, it is in my sack!" Their hearts failed them, and they turned trembling to one another, saying, "What is this that out God has done to us?" ²⁹They came to Jacob(*Heel grabber*) their father, to the land of Canaan(*Brought low*), and told him all that had happened to them, saying, ³⁰"The man, the lord of the land, spoke roughly with us, and took us for spies of the country. ³¹We said to him, 'We are honest men. We are no spies. ³²We are twelve brothers, sons of our father; one is no more, and the youngest is today with our father in the land of Canaan(*Brought low*).' ³³The man, the lord of the land, said to us, 'By this I will know that you are honest men: leave one of your brothers with me, and take grain for the famine of your houses, and go your way. ³⁴Bring your youngest brother to me. Then I will know that you are not spies, but that you are honest men. So I will deliver your brother to you, and you will trade in the land.'" ³⁵As they emptied their sacks, behold, each man's bundle of money was in his sack. When they and their father saw their bundles of money, they were afraid. ³⁶Jacob(*Heel grabber*), their father, said to them, "You have bereaved me of my children! Joseph(*May He add*) is no more, Simeon(*One who heard and obeyed*) is no more, and you want to take Benjamin(*Son of my right hand*) away. All these things are against me." ³⁷Reuben(*I see a son!*) spoke to his father, saying, "Kill my two sons, if I do not bring him to you. Entrust him to my care, and I will bring him to you again." ³⁸He said, "My son will not go down with you; for his brother is dead, and he only is left. If harm happens to him along the way in which you go, then you will bring down my gray hairs with sorrow to Sheol(*Asked for*)."

CHAPTER 43

¹The famine was severe in the land. ²When they had eaten up the grain which they had brought out of Egypt(*Double anxiety*), their father said to them, "Go again, buy us a little more food." ³Judah(*One who praises*) spoke to him, saying, "The man solemnly warned us, saying, 'You will not see my face, unless your brother is with you.' ⁴If you'll send our brother with us, we'll go down and buy you food, ⁵but if you'll not send him, we'll not go down, for the man said to us, 'You will not see my face, unless your brother is with you.'" ⁶Israel(*Struggler with God*) said, "Why did you treat me so badly, telling the man that you had another brother?" ⁷They said, "The man asked directly concerning ourselves, and concerning our relatives, saying, 'Is your father still alive? Have you another brother?' We just answered his questions. Is there any way we could know that he would say, 'Bring your brother down?'" ⁸Judah(*One who praises*) said to Israel(*Struggler with God*), his father, "Send the boy with me, and we'll get up and go, so that we may live, and not die, both we, and you, and also our little ones. ⁹I'll be collateral for him. From my hand will you require him. If I do not bring him to you, and set him before you, then let me bear the blame forever, ¹⁰for if we hadn't delayed, surely we would have returned a second time by now." ¹¹Their father, Israel(*Struggler with God*), said to them, "If it must be so, then do this. Take from the choice fruits of the land in your bags, and carry down a present for the man, a little balm, a little honey, spices and myrrh, nuts, and almonds; ¹²and take double money in your hand, and take back the money that was returned in the mouth of your sacks. Perhaps it was an oversight. ¹³Take your brother also, get up, and return to the man. ¹⁴May the God who is enough give you mercy before the man, that he may release to you your other brother and Benjamin(*Son of my right hand*). If I am bereaved of my children, I am bereaved." ¹⁵The men took that present, and they took double money in their hand, and Benjamin(*Son of my right hand);* and got up, went down to Egypt(*Double anxiety*), and stood before Joseph(*May He add*). ¹⁶When Joseph(*May

He add) saw Benjamin(*Son of my right hand*) with them, he said to the steward of his house, "Bring the men into the house, and butcher an animal, and prepare; for the men will dine with me at noon." ¹⁷The man did as Joseph(*May He add*) commanded, and the man brought the men to the house of Joseph(*May He add*). ¹⁸The men were afraid, because they were brought to the house of Joseph(*May He add*); and they said, "Because of the money that was returned in our sacks at the first time, we're brought in; that he may seek occasion against us, attack us, and seize us as slaves, along with our donkeys." ¹⁹They came near to the steward of the house of Joseph(*May He add*), and they spoke to him at the door of the house, ²⁰and said, "Oh, my lord, we indeed came down the first time to buy food. ²¹When we came to the lodging place, we opened our sacks, and behold, each man's money was in the mouth of his sack, our money in full weight. We have brought it back in our hand. ²²We have brought down other money in our hand to buy food. We do not know who put our money in our sacks." ²³He said, "Peace be to you. Do not be afraid. Our God, and the God of your father, has given you treasure in your sacks. I received your money." He brought Simeon-(*One who heard and obeyed*) out to them. ²⁴The man brought the men into the house of Joseph(*May He add*) house, and gave them water, and they washed their feet. He gave their donkeys fodder. ²⁵They prepared the present for the coming of Joseph(*May He add*) at noon, for they heard that they should eat bread there. ²⁶When Joseph(*May He add*) came home, they brought him the present which was in their hand into the house, and bowed themselves down to him to the earth. ²⁷He asked them of their welfare, and said, "Is your father well, the old man of whom you spoke? Is he yet alive?" ²⁸They said, "Your servant, our father, is well. He is still alive." They bowed down humbly. ²⁹He lifted up his eyes, and saw Benjamin(*Son of my right hand*), his brother, his mother's son, and said, "Is this your youngest brother, of whom you spoke to me?" He said, "Our God be gracious to you, my son." ³⁰Joseph(*May He add*) hurried, for his heart yearned over his brother; and he sought a place to weep. He entered into his room, and wept there. ³¹He washed his face, and came out. He controlled himself, and said, "Serve the meal." ³²They served him by himself, and them by themselves, and the Egyptians(*Much anxious ones*), that ate with him, by themselves, because the Egyptians(*Much anxious ones*) do not eat bread with the Hebrews(*Ones passing over*), for that is an abomination to the Egyptians(*Much anxious ones*). ³³They sat before him, the firstborn according to his birthright, and the youngest according to his youth, and the men marveled one with another. ³⁴He sent portions to them from before him, but the portion of Benjamin(*Son of my right hand*) was five times as much as any of theirs. They drank, and were merry with him.

CHAPTER 44

¹He commanded the steward of his house, saying, "Fill the men's sacks with food, as much as they can carry, and put each man's money in his sack's mouth. ²Put my cup, the silver cup, in the sack's mouth of the youngest, with his grain money." He did according to the word that Joseph(*May He add*) had spoken. ³As soon as the morning was light, the men were sent away, they and their donkeys. ⁴When they had gone out of the city, and were not yet far off, Joseph(*May He add*) said to his steward, "Up, follow after the men. When you overtake them, ask them, 'Why have you rewarded evil for good? ⁵Is not this that from which my lord drinks, and by which he indeed divines? You have done evil in so doing.'" ⁶He overtook them, and he spoke these words to them. ⁷They said to him, "Why does my lord speak such words as these? Far be it from your servants that they should do such a thing! ⁸Behold, the money, which we found in our sacks' mouths, we brought again to you out of the land of Canaan(*Brought low*). How then should we steal silver or gold out of your lord's house? ⁹With whomever of your servants it is found, let him die, and we also will be my lord's slaves." ¹⁰He said, "Now also let it be according to your words: he with whom it is found will be my slave; and you will be blameless." ¹¹Then they hurried, and each man took his sack down to the ground, and each man opened his sack. ¹²He searched, beginning with the oldest, and ending at the youngest. The cup was found in the sack of Benjamin(*Son of my right hand*). ¹³Then they tore their clothes, and each man loaded his donkey, and returned to the city. ¹⁴Judah(*One who praises*) and his brothers came to the house of Joseph(*May He add*), and he was still there. They fell on the ground before him. ¹⁵Joseph(*May He add*) said to them, "What deed is this that you have done? Do not you know that such a man as I can indeed practice divination?" ¹⁶Judah(*One who praises*) said, "What will we tell my lord? What will we speak? Or how will we clear ourselves? Our God has found out the iniquity of your servants. Behold, we are my lord's slaves, both we, and he also in whose hand the cup is found." ¹⁷He said, "Far be it from

me that I should do so. The man in whose hand the cup is found, he will be my slave; but as for you, go up in peace to your father." ¹⁸Then Judah(*One who praises*) came near to him, and said, "Oh, my lord, please let your servant speak a word in my lord's ears, and do not let your anger burn against your servant; for you are even as Pharaoh. ¹⁹My lord asked his servants, saying, 'Have you a father, or a brother?' ²⁰We said to my lord, 'We have a father, an old man, and a child of his old age, a little one; and his brother is dead, and he alone is left of his mother; and his father loves him.' ²¹You said to your servants, 'Bring him down to me, that I may set my eyes on him.' ²²We said to my lord, 'The boy cannot leave his father: for if he should leave his father, his father would die.' ²³You said to your servants, 'Unless your youngest brother comes down with you, you will see my face no more.' ²⁴When we came up to your servant my father, we told him the words of my lord. ²⁵Our father said, 'Go again, buy us a little food.' ²⁶We said, 'We cannot go down. If our youngest brother is with us, then we will go down: for we may not see the man's face, unless our youngest brother is with us.' ²⁷Your servant, my father, said to us, 'You know that my wife bore me two sons: ²⁸and the one went out from me, and I said, "Surely he is torn in pieces"; and I have not seen him since. ²⁹If you take this one also from me, and harm happens to him, you will bring down my gray hairs with sorrow to Sheol(*Asked for*).' ³⁰Now therefore when I come to your servant my father, and the boy is not with us; since his life is bound up in the boy's life; ³¹it will happen, when he sees that the boy is no more, that he will die. Your servants will bring down the gray hairs of your servant, our father, with sorrow to Sheol(*Asked for*). ³²For your servant became collateral for the boy to my father, saying, 'If I do not bring him to you, then I will bear the blame to my father forever.' ³³Now therefore, please let your servant stay instead of the boy, my lord's slave; and let the boy go up with his brothers. ³⁴For how will I go up to my father, if the boy is not with me?—unless I see the evil that will come on my father."

CHAPTER 45

¹Then Joseph(*May He add*) could not control himself before all those who stood before him, and he cried, "Cause everyone to go out from me!" No one else stood with him, while Joseph(*May He add*) made himself known to his brothers. ²He wept aloud. The Egyptians(*Much anxious ones*) heard, and the house of Pharaoh heard. ³Joseph(*May He add*) said to his brothers, "I am Joseph(*May He add*)! Does my father still live?" His brothers could not answer him; for they were terrified at his presence. ⁴Joseph(*May He add*) said to his brothers, "Come near to me, please." They came near. "He said, I am Joseph(*May He add*), your brother, whom you sold into Egypt(*Double anxiety*). ⁵Now do not be grieved, nor angry with yourselves, that you sold me here, for our God sent me before you to preserve life. ⁶For these two years the famine has been in the land, and there are yet five years, in which there will be no plowing and no harvest. ⁷Our God sent me before you to preserve for you a remnant in the earth, and to save you alive by a great deliverance. ⁸So now it was not you who sent me here, but our God, and he has made me a father to Pharaoh, lord of all his house, and ruler over all the land of Egypt(*Double anxiety*). ⁹Hurry, and go up to my father, and tell him, 'This is what your son Joseph(*May He add*) says, "Our God has made me lord of all Egypt(*Double anxiety*). Come down to me. Do not wait. ¹⁰You will dwell in the land of Goshen(*Drawing near*), and you will be near to me, you, your children, your children's children, your flocks, your herds, and all that you have. ¹¹There I will nourish you; for there are yet five years of famine; unless you come to poverty, you, and your household, and all that you have.'" ¹²Behold, your eyes see, and the eyes of my brother Benjamin(*Son of my right hand*), that it is my mouth that speaks to you. ¹³You will tell my father of all my glory in Egypt(*Double anxiety*), and of all that you have seen. You will hurry and bring my father down here." ¹⁴He fell on the neck of his brother Benjamin(*Son of my right hand*), and wept, and Benjamin(*Son of my right hand*) wept on his neck. ¹⁵He kissed all his brothers, and wept on them. After that his brothers talked with him. ¹⁶The re-

port of it was heard in Pharaoh's house, saying, "The brothers of Joseph(*May He add*) have come." It pleased Pharaoh well, and his servants. ¹⁷Pharaoh said to Joseph(*May He add*), "Tell your brothers, 'Do this. Load your animals, and go, travel to the land of Canaan(*Brought low*). ¹⁸Take your father and your households, and come to me, and I will give you the good of the land of Egypt(*Double anxiety*), and you will eat the fat of the land.' ¹⁹Now you are commanded: do this. Take wagons out of the land of Egypt(*Double anxiety*) for your little ones, and for your wives, and bring your father, and come. ²⁰Also, do not concern yourselves about your belongings, for the good of all the land of Egypt(*Double anxiety*) is yours." ²¹The sons of Israel(*Struggler with God*) did so. Joseph(*May He add*) gave them wagons, according to the commandment of Pharaoh, and gave them provision for the way. ²²He gave each one of them changes of clothing, but to Benjamin(*Son of my right hand*) he gave three hundred pieces of silver and five changes of clothing. ²³He sent the following to his father: ten donkeys loaded with the good things of Egypt(*Double anxiety*), and ten female donkeys loaded with grain and bread and provision for his father by the way. ²⁴So he sent his brothers away, and they departed. He said to them, "See that you do not quarrel on the way." ²⁵They went up out of Egypt(*Double anxiety*), and came into the land of Canaan(*Brought low*), to Jacob(*Heel grabber*) their father. ²⁶They told him, saying, "Joseph(*May He add*) is still alive, and he is ruler over all the land of Egypt(*Double anxiety*)." His heart fainted, for he did not believe them. ²⁷They told him all the words of Joseph(*May He add*), which he had said to them. When he saw the wagons which Joseph(*May He add*) had sent to carry him, the spirit of Jacob(*Heel grabber*), their father, revived. ²⁸Israel(*Struggler with God*) said, "It is enough. Joseph(*May He add*) my son is still alive. I will go and see him before I die."

CHAPTER 46

¹Israel(*Struggler with God*) traveled with all that he had, and came to Beersheba(*Well of oath*), and offered sacrifices to the God of his father, Isaac(*Laughter*). ²Our God spoke to Israel(*Struggler with God*) in the visions of the night, and said, "Jacob(*Heel grabber*), Jacob(*Heel grabber*)!" He said, "Here I am." ³He said, "I am God, the God of your father. Do not be afraid to go down into Egypt(*Double anxiety*), for there I will make of you a great nation. ⁴I will go down with you into Egypt(*Double anxiety*). I will also surely bring you up again. Joseph(*May He add*) will close your eyes." ⁵Jacob(*Heel grabber*) rose up from Beersheba(*Well of Oath*), and the sons of Israel(*Struggler with God*) carried Jacob(*Heel grabber*), their father, their little ones, and their wives, in the wagons which Pharaoh had sent to carry him. ⁶They took their livestock, and their goods, which they had gotten in the land of Canaan(*Brought low*), and came into Egypt(*Double anxiety*)—Jacob(*Heel grabber*), and all his offspring with him, ⁷his sons, and his sons' sons with him, his daughters, and his sons' daughters, and he brought all his offspring with him into Egypt(*Double anxiety*). ⁸These are the names of the children of Israel(*Struggler with God*), who came into Egypt(*Double anxiety*), Jacob(*Heel grabber*) and his sons: Reuben(*I see a son!*), the firstborn of Jacob(*Heel grabber*). ⁹The sons of Reuben(*I see a son!*): Hanoch(*Dedicate*), Pallu(*Different*), Hezron(*Enclosure*), and Carmi(*My vineyard*). ¹⁰The sons of Simeon(*One who heard and obeyed*): Jemuel(*Day of God*), Jamin(*Right hand*), Ohad(*Together in covenant*), Jachin(*He will establish*), Zohar(*Whiteness*), and Shaul(*Asked for*) the son of a Canaanite(*One brought low*) woman. ¹¹The sons of Levi(*Attached*): Gershon(*A stranger there*), Kohath(*Obedient one*), and Merari(*My bitterness*). ¹²The sons of Judah(*One who praises*): Er(*Awaken to watch*), Onan(*Their trouble*), Shelah(*Prayer*), Perez(*Breakthrough*), and Zerah(*Rising*); but Er(*Awaken to watch*) and Onan(*Their trouble*) died in the land of Canaan(*Brought low*). The sons of Perez(*Breakthrough*) were Hezron(*Enclosure*) and Hamul(*One pitied*). ¹³The sons of Issachar(*Hired for wage*): Tola(*Purple worm*), Puvah(*Broken apart*), Yob(*One perse-

cuted), and Shimron(*Vigiliant guard*). ¹⁴The sons of Zebulun(*Glorious dwelling*): Sered(*One who escapes*), Elon(*Mighty oak*), and Jahleel(*Hope in God*). ¹⁵These are the sons of Leah(*Wearied*), whom she bore to Jacob(*Heel grabber*) in Paddan-Aram(*Elevated plain*), with his daughter Dinah(*Lover of justice*). All the souls of his sons and his daughters were thirty-three. ¹⁶The sons of Gad(*Fortunate*): Ziphion(*Watchman*), Haggi(*Born on a feast day*), Shuni(*My ease*), Ezbon(*Great beauty*), Eri(*My watcher*), Arodi(*My posterity*), and Areli(*Lion of my God*). ¹⁷The sons of Asher(*Happy*): Imnah(*Right-hand side*), Ishvah(*He will level*), Ishvi(*He is my equal*), Beriah(*Trouble*), and Serah(*Abundance*) their sister. The sons of Beriah *(Trouble)*: Heber(*Associate*) and Malchiel(*My King is God*). ¹⁸These are the sons of Zilpah(*A drop*), whom Laban(*White*) gave to Leah(*Wearied*), his daughter, and these she bore to Jacob(*Heel grabber*), even sixteen souls. ¹⁹The sons of Rachel(*Lamb*), wife of Jacob(*Heel grabber*): Joseph(*May He add*) and Benjamin(*Son of my right hand*). ²⁰To Joseph(*May He add*) in the land of Egypt(*Double anxiety*) were born Manasseh(*Made to forget*) and Ephraim(*Very fruitful*), whom Asenath(*Mischief*), the daughter of Potiphera(*Whom the sun god gave*), priest of On(*Pillar*), bore him. ²¹The sons of Benjamin(*Son of my right hand*): Bela(*Devouring*), Becher(*Firstborn*), Ashbel(*Vain fire*), Gera(*Chewing cud*), Naaman(*Pleasant one*), Ehi(*My brother*), Rosh(*Head*), Muppim(*Dying gasps*), Huppim(*Coverings*), and Ard(*Fugitive*). ²²These are the sons of Rachel(*Lamb*), who were born to Jacob(*Heel grabber*): all the souls were fourteen. ²³The son of Dan(*One who judges*): Hushim(*Hurried ones*). ²⁴The sons of Naphtali(*My struggle*): Jahzeel(*God portioned*), Guni(*My garden*), Jezer(*One who forms*), and Shillem(*Payback*). ²⁵These are the sons of Bilhah(*Troubled*), whom Laban(*White*) gave to Rachel(*Lamb*), his daughter, and these she bore to Jacob(*Heel grabber*): all the souls were seven. ²⁶All the souls who came with Jacob(*Heel grabber*) into Egypt(*Double anxiety*), who were his direct offspring, besides the son's wives of Jacob(*Heel grabber*), all the souls were sixty-six. ²⁷The sons of Joseph(*May He add*), who were born to him in Egypt(*Double anxiety*), were two souls. All the souls of the house of Jacob(*Heel grabber*), who came into Egypt(*Double anxiety*), were seventy. ²⁸He sent Judah(*One who praises*) before him to Joseph(*May He add*), to show the way before him to Goshen(*Drawing near*), and they came into the land of Goshen(*Drawing near*). ²⁹Joseph(*May He add*) prepared his chariot, and went up to meet Israel(*Struggler with God*), his father, in Goshen(*Drawing near*). He presented himself to him, and fell on his neck, and wept on his neck a good while. ³⁰Israel(*Struggler with God*) said to Joseph(*May He add*), "Now let me die, since I have seen your face, that you are still alive." ³¹Joseph(*May He add*) said to his brothers, and to his father's house, "I will go up, and speak with Pharaoh, and will tell him, 'My brothers, and my father's house, who were in the land of Canaan(*Brought low*), have come to me. ³²These men are shepherds, for they have been keepers of livestock, and they have brought their flocks, and their herds, and all that they have.' ³³It will happen, when Pharaoh summons you, and will say, 'What is your occupation?' ³⁴ that you will say, 'Your servants have been keepers of livestock from our youth even until now, both we, and our fathers:' that you may dwell in the land of Goshen(*Drawing near*); for every shepherd is an abomination to the Egyptians(*Much anxious ones*)."

CHAPTER 47

¹Then Joseph(*May He add*) went in and told Pharaoh, and said, "My father and my brothers, with their flocks, their herds, and all that they own, have come out of the land of Canaan(*Brought low*); and behold, they are in the land of Goshen(*Drawing near*)." ²From among his brothers he took five men, and presented them to Pharaoh. ³Pharaoh said to his brothers, "What is your occupation?" They said to Pharaoh, "Your servants are shepherds, both we, and our fathers." ⁴They said to Pharaoh, "We have come to live as foreigners in the land, for there is no pasture for your servants' flocks because the famine is severe in the land of Canaan(*Brought low*). Now therefore, please let your servants dwell in the land of Goshen(*Drawing near*)." ⁵Pharaoh spoke to Joseph(*May He add*), saying, "Your father and your brothers have come to you. ⁶The land of Egypt(*Double anxiety*) is before you. Make your father and your brothers dwell in the best of the land. Let them dwell in the land of Goshen(*Drawing near*). If you know any able men among them, then put them in charge of my livestock." ⁷Joseph(*May He add*) brought in Jacob(*Heel grabber*), his father, and set him before Pharaoh, and Jacob(*Heel grabber*) blessed Pharaoh. ⁸Pharaoh said to Jacob(*Heel grabber*), "How many are the days of the years of your life?" ⁹Jacob(*Heel grabber*) said to Pharaoh, "The days of the years of my pilgrimage are one hundred thirty years. Few and evil have been the days of the years of my life, and they have not attained to the days of the years of the life of my fathers in the days of their pilgrimage." ¹⁰Jacob(*Heel grabber*) blessed Pharaoh, and went out from the presence of Pharaoh. ¹¹Joseph(*May He add*) placed his father and his brothers, and gave them a possession in the land of Egypt(*Double anxiety*), in the best of the land, in the land of Rameses(*Born of the sun*), as Pharaoh had commanded. ¹²Joseph(*May He add*) nourished his father, his brothers, and all of his father's household, with bread, according to their families. ¹³There was no bread in all the land; for the famine was very severe, so that the land of Egypt(*Double anxiety*) and the land of Canaan(*Brought low*) fainted by reason of the famine. ¹⁴Joseph(

May He add) gathered up all the money that was found in the land of Egypt(*Double anxiety*), and in the land of Canaan(*Brought low*), for the grain which they bought: and Joseph(*May He add*) brought the money into Pharaoh's house. ¹⁵When the money was all spent in the land of Egypt(*Double anxiety*), and in the land of Canaan(*Brought low*), all the Egyptians(*Much anxious ones*) came to Joseph(*May He add*), and said, "Give us bread, for why should we die in your presence? For our money fails." ¹⁶Joseph(*May He add*) said, "Give me your livestock; and I will give you food for your livestock, if your money is gone." ¹⁷They brought their livestock to Joseph(*May He add*), and Joseph(*May He add*) gave them bread in exchange for the horses, and for the flocks, and for the herds, and for the donkeys: and he fed them with bread in exchange for all their livestock for that year. ¹⁸When that year was ended, they came to him the second year, and said to him, "We will not hide from my lord how our money is all spent, and the herds of livestock are my lord's. There is nothing left in the sight of my lord, but our bodies, and our lands. ¹⁹Why should we die before your eyes, both we and our land? Buy us and our land for bread, and we and our land will be servants to Pharaoh. Give us seed, that we may live, and not die, and that the land will not be desolate." ²⁰So Joseph(*May He add*) bought all the land of Egypt(*Double anxiety*) for Pharaoh, for every man of the Egyptians(*Much anxious ones*) sold his field, because the famine was severe on them, and the land became Pharaoh's. ²¹As for the people, he moved them to the cities from one end of the border of Egypt(*Double anxiety*) even to the other end of it. ²²Only he did not buy the land of the priests, for the priests had a portion from Pharaoh, and ate their portion which Pharaoh gave them. That is why they did not sell their land. ²³Then Joseph(*May He add*) said to the people, "Behold, I have bought you and your land today for Pharaoh. Behold, here is seed for you, and you will sow the land. ²⁴It will happen at the harvests, that you will give a fifth to Pharaoh, and four parts will be your own, for seed of the field, for your food, for them of your households, and for food for your little ones." ²⁵They said, "You have saved our lives! Let us find favor in the sight of my lord, and we will be Pharaoh's servants." ²⁶Joseph(*May He add*) made it a principle concerning the land of Egypt(*Double anxiety*) to this day, that Pharaoh should have the fifth. Only the land of the priests alone did not become Pharaoh's. ²⁷Israel(*Struggler with God*) lived in the land of Egypt(*Double anxiety*), in the land of Goshen(*Drawing near*);

and they got themselves possessions therein, and were fruitful, and multiplied exceedingly. ²⁸Jacob(*Heel grabber*) lived in the land of Egypt(*Double anxiety*) seventeen years. So the days of Jacob(*Heel grabber*), the years of his life, were one hundred forty-seven years. ²⁹The time came near that Israel(*Struggler with God*) must die, and he called his son Joseph(*May He add*), and said to him, "If now I have found favor in your sight, please put your hand under my thigh, and deal kindly and truly with me. Please do not bury me in Egypt(*Double anxiety*), ³⁰but when I sleep with my fathers, you will carry me out of Egypt(*Double anxiety*), and bury me in their burying place." He said, "I will do as you have said." ³¹He said, "Swear to me," and he swore to him. Israel(*Struggler with God*) bowed himself on the bed's head.

CHAPTER 48

¹After these things, someone said to Joseph(*May He add*), "Behold, your father is sick." He took with him his two sons, Manasseh(*Made to forget*) and Ephraim(*Very fruitful*). ² Someone told Jacob(*Heel grabber*), and said, "Behold, your son Joseph(*May He add*) comes to you," and Israel(*Struggler with God*) strengthened himself, and sat on the bed. ³Jacob(*Heel grabber*) said to Joseph(*May He add*), "Our God who is enough appeared to me at Luz(*Almond tree*) in the land of Canaan(*Brought low*), and blessed me, ⁴and said to me, 'Behold, I will make you fruitful, and multiply you, and I will make of you a company of peoples, and will give this land to your offspring after you for an everlasting possession.' ⁵Now your two sons, who were born to you in the land of Egypt(*Double anxiety*) before I came to you into Egypt(*Double anxiety*), are mine; Ephraim(*Very fruitful*) and Manasseh(*Made to forget*), even as Reuben(*I see a son!*) and Simeon(*One who heard and obeyed*), will be mine. ⁶Your issue, whom you become the father of after them, will be yours. They will be called after the name of their brothers in their inheritance. ⁷As for me, when I came from Paddan(*Plain*), Rachel(*Lamb*) died by me in the land of Canaan(*Brought low*) on the way, when there was still some distance to come to Ephrath(*Fruitful land*), and I buried her there on the way to Ephrath(*Fruitful land*) [also called Bethlehem (*House of bread*)]." ⁸Israel(*Struggler with God*) saw the sons of Joseph(*May He add*), and said, "Who are these?" ⁹Joseph(*May He add*) said to his father, "They are my sons, whom our God has given me here." He said, "Please bring them to me, and I will bless them." ¹⁰Now the eyes of Israel(*Struggler with God*) were dim for age, so that he could not see. He brought them near to him; and he kissed them, and embraced them. ¹¹Israel(*Struggler with God*) said to Joseph(*May He add*), "I did not think I would see your face, and behold, our God has let me see your offspring also." ¹²Joseph(*May He add*) brought them out from between his knees, and he bowed himself with his face to the earth. ¹³Joseph(*May He add*) took them both, Ephraim(*Very fruitful*) in his right hand toward the left hand of Is-

rael(*Struggler with God*), and Manasseh(*Made to forget*) in his left hand toward the right hand of Israel(*Struggler with God*), and brought them near to him. ¹⁴Israel(*Struggler with God*) stretched out his right hand, and laid it on the head of Ephraim(*Very fruitful*), who was the younger, and his left hand on the head of Manasseh(*Made to forget*), guiding his hands knowingly, for Manasseh(*Made to forget*) was the firstborn. ¹⁵He blessed Joseph(*May He add*), and said, "The God before whom my fathers Abraham(*Father of nations*) and Isaac(*Laughter*) walked, the God who has fed me all my life long to this day, ¹⁶the angel who has redeemed me from all evil, bless the lads, and let my name be named on them, and the name of my fathers Abraham(*Father of nations*) and Isaac(*Laughter*). Let them grow into a multitude upon the earth." ¹⁷When Joseph(*May He add*) saw that his father laid his right hand on the head of Ephraim(*Very fruitful*), it displeased him. He held up his father's hand, to remove it from head of Ephraim(*Very fruitful*) to the head of Manasseh(*Made to forget*). ¹⁸Joseph(*May He add*) said to his father, "Not so, my father; for this is the firstborn; put your right hand on his head." ¹⁹His father refused, and said, "I know, my son, I know. He also will become a people, and he also will be great. However, his younger brother will be greater than he, and his offspring will become a multitude of nations." ²⁰He blessed them that day, saying, "In you will Israel(*Struggler with God*) bless, saying, 'Our God make you as Ephraim(*Very fruitful*) and as Manasseh(*Made to forget*)'" He set Ephraim(*Very fruitful*) before Manasseh(*Made to forget*). ²¹Israel(*Struggler with God*) said to Joseph(*May He add*), "Behold, I am dying, but our God will be with you, and bring you again to the land of your fathers. ²²Moreover I have given to you one portion above your brothers, which I took out of the hand of the Amorite(*Hill dweller*) with my sword and with my bow."

CHAPTER 49

¹Jacob(*Heel grabber*) called to his sons, and said: "Gather yourselves together, that I may tell you that which will happen to you in the days to come. ²Assemble yourselves, and hear, you sons of Jacob(*Heel grabber*). Listen to Israel(*Struggler with God*), your father ³Reuben(*I see a son!*), you are my firstborn, my might, and the beginning of my strength; excelling in dignity, and excelling in power. ⁴Boiling over like water, you will not excel; because you went up to your father's bed, then defiled it. He went up to my couch. ⁵Simeon(*One who heard and obeyed*) and Levi(*Attached*) are brothers. Their swords are weapons of violence. ⁶My soul, do not come into their council. My glory, do not be united to their assembly; for in their anger they killed men. In their self-will they hamstrung cattle. ⁷Cursed be their anger, for it was fierce; and their wrath, for it was cruel. I will divide them in Jacob(*Heel grabber*), and scatter them in Israel(*Struggler with God*). ⁸Judah(*One who praises*), your brothers will praise you. Your hand will be on the neck of your enemies. Your father's sons will bow down before you. ⁹Judah(*One who praises*) is a lion's cub. From the prey, my son, you have gone up. He stooped down, he crouched as a lion, as a lioness. Who will rouse him up? ¹⁰The scepter will not depart from Judah(*One who praises*), nor the ruler's staff from between his feet, until He comes to whom it belongs. To him will the obedience of the peoples be. ¹¹Binding his foal to the vine, his donkey's colt to the choice vine; he has washed his garments in wine, his robes in the blood of grapes. ¹²His eyes will be red with wine, his teeth white with milk. ¹³Zebulun(*Glorious dwelling*) will dwell at the haven of the sea. He will be for a haven of ships. His border will be on Sidon(*Place to fish*). ¹⁴Issachar(*Hired for wage*) is a strong donkey, lying down between the saddlebags. ¹⁵He saw a resting place, that it was good, the land, that it was pleasant. He bows his shoulder to the burden, and becomes a servant doing forced labor. ¹⁶Dan(*One who judges*) will judge his people, as one of the tribes of Israel(*Struggler with God*). ¹⁷Dan(*One who judges*) will be a serpent on the trail, an adder in the path,

that bites the horse's heels, so that his rider falls backward. ¹⁸I have waited for your salvation, Yahweh(*Jealous one*). ¹⁹A troop will press on Gad (*Fortunate*),but he will press on their heel. ²⁰The food of Asher(*Happy*) will be rich. He will produce royal dainties. ²¹Naphtali(*My struggle*) is a doe set free, who bears beautiful fawns. ²²Joseph(*May He add*) is a fruitful vine,a fruitful vine by a spring. His branches run over the wall. ²³The archers have severely grieved him, shot at him, and persecute him: ²⁴But his bow remained strong. The arms of his hands were made strong, by the hands of the Mighty One of Jacob(*Heel grabber*), [from there is the shepherd, the stone of Israel(*Struggler with God*)], ²⁵even by the God of your father, who will help you; by the God who is enough, who will bless you, with blessings of heaven above, blessings of the deep that lies below, blessings of the breasts, and of the womb.²⁶The blessings of your father have prevailed above the blessings of your ancestors, above the boundaries of the ancient hills. They will be on the head of Joseph(*May He add*), on the crown of the head of him who is separated from his brothers. ²⁷Benjamin(*Son of my right hand*) is a ravenous wolf. In the morning he will devour the prey. At evening he will divide the plunder." ²⁸All these are the twelve tribes of Israel(*Struggler with God*), and this is what their father spoke to them and blessed them. He blessed everyone according to his blessing. ²⁹He instructed them, and said to them, "I am to be gathered to my people. Bury me with my fathers in the cave that is in the field of Ephron(*Antelope*) the Hittite (*Terrorist*), ³⁰in the cave that is in the field of Machpelah(*One above another*), which is before Mamre(*Revealed from seeing*), in the land of Canaan(*Brought low*), which Abraham(*Father of nations*) bought with the field from Ephron(*Antelope*) the Hittite(*Terrorist*) as a burial place. ³¹There they buried Abraham(*Father of nations*) and Sarah(*Daughter destined to rule*), his wife. There they buried Isaac(*Laughter*) and Rebekah(*Securely bound*), his wife, and there I buried Leah(*Wearied*): ³²the field and the cave that is therein, which was purchased from the children of Heth(*Exhausted*)." ³³When Jacob(*Heel grabber*) finished charging his sons, he gathered up his feet into the bed, and yielded up the spirit, and was gathered to his people.

CHAPTER 50

¹Joseph(*May He add*) fell on his father's face, wept on him, and kissed him. ²Joseph(*May He add*) commanded his servants, the physicians, to embalm his father; and the physicians embalmed Israel(*Struggler with God*). ³Forty days were fulfilled for him, for that is how many the days it takes to embalm. The Egyptians(*Much anxious ones*) wept for him for seventy days. ⁴When the days of weeping for him were past, Joseph(*May He add*) spoke to the house of Pharaoh, saying, "If now I have found favor in your eyes, please speak in the ears of Pharaoh, saying, ⁵'My father made me swear, saying, "Behold, I am dying. Bury me in my grave which I have dug for myself in the land of Canaan(*Brought low*)." Now therefore, please let me go up and bury my father, and I will come again.'" ⁶Pharaoh said, "Go up, and bury your father, just like he made you swear." ⁷Joseph(*May He add*) went up to bury his father; and with him went up all the servants of Pharaoh, the elders of his house, all the elders of the land of Egypt(*Double anxiety*), ⁸all the house of Joseph(*May He add*), his brothers, and his father's house. Only their little ones, their flocks, and their herds, they left in the land of Goshen(*Drawing near*). ⁹There went up with him both chariots and horsemen. It was a very great company. ¹⁰They came to the threshing floor of Atad(*Thornbush*), which is beyond the Jordan(*Descending*), and there they lamented with a very great and severe lamentation. He mourned for his father seven days. ¹¹When the inhabitants of the land, the Canaanites(*Ones brought low*), saw the mourning in the floor of Atad(*Thornbush*), they said, "This is a grievous mourning by the Egyptians(*Much anxious ones*)." Therefore its name was called Abel-Mizraim(*Vapor of double anxiety*) which is beyond the Jordan (*Descending*). ¹²His sons did to him just as he commanded them, ¹³for his sons carried him into the land of Canaan(*Brought low*), and buried him in the cave of the field of Machpelah(*One above another*), which Abraham(*Father of nations*) bought with the field, for a possession of a burial site, from Ephron(*Antelope*) the Hittite(*Terrorist*), before Mamre(*Revealed from seeing*). ¹⁴Joseph(*May He add*) re-

turned into Egypt(*Double anxiety*)—he, and his brothers, and all that went up with him to bury his father, after he had buried his father. ¹⁵When the brothers of Joseph(*May He add*) saw that their father was dead, they said, "It may be that Joseph(*May He add*) will hate us, and will fully pay us back for all the evil which we did to him." ¹⁶They sent a message to Joseph(*May He add*), saying, "Your father commanded before he died, saying, ¹⁷'You will tell Joseph(*May He add*), now please forgive the disobedience of your brothers, and their sin, because they did evil to you.'" Now, please forgive the disobedience of the servants of the God of your father." Joseph(*May He add*) wept when they spoke to him. ¹⁸His brothers also went and fell down before his face; and they said, "Behold, we are your servants." ¹⁹Joseph(*May He add*) said to them, "Do not be afraid, for am I in the place of our God? ²⁰As for you, you meant evil against me, but our God meant it for good, to bring to pass, as it is today, to save many people alive. ²¹Now therefore do not be afraid. I will nourish you and your little ones." He comforted them, and spoke kindly to them. ²²Joseph(*May He add*) lived in Egypt(*Double anxiety*), he, and his father's house. Joseph(*May He add*) lived one hundred ten years. ²³Joseph(*May He add*) saw the children of Ephraim(*Very fruitful*) to the third generation. The children also of Machir(*Purchased*), the son of Manasseh(*Made to forget*), were born on the knees of Joseph(*May He add*). ²⁴Joseph(*May He add*) said to his brothers, "I am dying, but our God will surely visit you, and bring you up out of this land to the land which he swore to Abraham(*Father of nations*), to Isaac (*Laughter*), and to Jacob(*Heel grabber*)." ²⁵Joseph(*May He add*) took an promise of the children of Israel(*Struggler with God*), saying, "Our God will surely visit you, and you will carry up my bones from here." ²⁶So Joseph(*May He add*) died, being one hundred ten years old, and they embalmed him, and he was put in a coffin in Egypt(*Double anxiety*).

ABOUT THE AUTHOR

Christopher Monaghan

Chris Monaghan and his wife, Debbie, live near Richmond, Indiana, U.S.A. Chris and Debbie are the Senior Leaders of a Gateway Church. Chris is also the co-founder of the Gateway Hunger Relief Center that feeds over 5000 families each month in his region. Chris believes in equipping every believer to do what Jesus did and his focus is on changing atmospheres of cities through worship, teaching and humanitarian acts. Chris has traveled to three continents, and regularly sees physical and emotional healings take place. Chris has authored six books and has written over 25 worship songs. Chris is a graduate of Penn State University, has a Master of Biblical Studies from Messiah Biblical Institute and has taught and studied at many other Seminaries and Bible schools. Chris and his wife Debbie also serve as coordinators for Family Foundations International and help facilitate emotional healing through their seminars. Chris and Debbie have five children and one grandchild. For speaking requests contact office@igateway.org. Go to www.igateway.org for more resources

PRAISE FOR AUTHOR

"The Name Translation Version is amazing! What a wonder work Pastor Chris Monaghan has given in restoring the meaning of the names found in the Bible!"
Dr. Brian Simmons
Lead Translator for the Passion Translation Project

BOOKS BY THIS AUTHOR

The Power Of Worship

This is a short, simple overview about our privilege to worship the King of the Universe. Many only worship when they feel right or the music sounds good or they are familiar with the song. Few realize the power available to all who will worship as an act of devotion- not just emotion. Throughout the Bible there are countless stories of miraculous breakthroughs that take place because of the realization that worship will shift the atmosphere wherever you are! The truths found in this book will help you bring heaven to earth on a daily basis.

Heaven's Dynasty

Have you ever been confused by the Trinity? Many great theologians have made this doctrine the centerpiece of our Christian faith. But most of us, truth be told, accept the Trinity as mystery because we have a hard time understanding it. The Trinity is an observation from a philosophical and scientific point of view that keeps one immune to heresy but few can explain it with confidence! Maybe we have overcomplicated things!
I believe God has a heart of simplicity. When Jesus walked the earth, He used everyday ideas that simple people like you and I could grasp. I have entitled this book "Heaven's Dynasty", and I believe this message will warm your heart and satisfy your soul. It is a journey that explains how the Trinity has upheld the most vital truth of Christianity for the last millennium and a half, but has inadvertently missed an important emphasis: the generational relationship between a Father and Son. This book is the story of how the Father is restoring the kingdom of God to earth through His Son Jesus!

Disturbing The Present Through Prayer

Got prayer? Often prayer is more obligation and guilt driven than joy and result driven. This book is my journey to pray with confidence and boldness. I have taught classes on prayer and preached countless messages on prayer, but I also pray daily and consistently because of the principles found in this writing. I want to share them with you and encourage you to read it and discover a fresh wind in your prayer journey. Prayer is a beautiful gift and compelling invitation that every child of God has been offered. If you want to change the future, you must disturb the present. Prayer creates a disturbance in the kingdom of darkness because it stirs up heaven to move. You and I have been invited into this position of privilege and honor. History belongs to us because we will pray and not give up.

Cities, Gates And Elders

Cities, Gates and Elders answers the question of why Jesus told Peter, "...upon this rock I will build my church; and the gates of hell shall not prevail against it" (Matthew 16:18). The disciples of Jesus understood that the gates were gateways in which the elders of the city would sit and judge. The decisions made at these gates had authoritative power over regions. Jesus was saying that the decisions made in hell would not prevail against the decisions made on earth by His people! Cities, Gates and Elders examines the deeper meaning of the Scriptures in light of the culture in which they were written, calling us to fulfill the ancient blessing, "And thy seed shall possess the gates of his enemies" (Genesis 22:17).

The Worship Handbook

The Worship Handbook is a 10 week course on how to live a life of worship and creative expression.

The Gates Of Nehemiah

The Gates of Nehemiah Study Guide is a journey around the gates of Jerusalem during the time of Nehemiah. Based on Nehemiah the third chapter, this study guide allows you to develop ten daily declarations and ten prayer focuses based upon each of the ten gates. Also available is an 11 week DVD study that gives an overview and a teaching on each gate.

Disturbing The Present Through Prayer Manual

Got prayer? Take this online course along with this manual to be equipped to pray. Often prayer is more obligation and guilt driven than joy and result driven. This book is my journey to pray with confidence and boldness. I have taught classes on prayer and preached countless messages on prayer, but I also pray daily and consistently because of the principles found in this writing. I want to share them with you and encourage you to read it and discover a fresh wind in your prayer journey. Prayer is a beautiful gift and compelling invitation that every child of God has been offered. If you want to change the future, you must disturb the present. Prayer creates a disturbance in the kingdom of darkness because it stirs up heaven to move. You and I have been invited into this position of privilege and honor. History belongs to us because we will pray and not give up.

Printed in Great Britain
by Amazon